HISTORY

OF THE

CHURCHES AND MINISTERS

CONNECTED WITH THE

PRESBYTERIAN AND CONGREGATIONAL

CONVENTION OF WISCONSIN,

AND OF THE OPERATIONS OF THE

AMERICAN HOME MISSIONARY SOCIETY

IN THE STATE,

FOR THE PAST TEN YEARS;

WITH AN APPENDIX.

BY REV. DEXTER CLARY.

BELOIT:
PRINTED BY B. E. HALE.

1861.

PREFACE.

This work is published by request of the Presbyterian and Congregational General Convention of Wisconsin.

The Committee of Publication, whose names are hereto annexed, was appointed by the Convention.

The labor of preparing it has devolved mainly on the Rev. Dexter Clary. It is the result of an extended statement made by him, as Agent of the American Home Missionary Society, to the Convention, of his labors the past ten years.

Deeming it important that the history of churches and ministers in our connection should be preserved, and that the great benefits received through the instrumentalily of Home Missions should be on record, the Agent was requested so to extend the statement as to make it answer these ends.

A similar History, extending from the first work of Home Missions, and the first organization of churches in Wisconsin, to the close of 1850, was prepared by Rev. Stephen Peet, the first Agent of the American Home Missionary Society on this field, and published by request of the Convention.

The present work commences where that closed, and is a continuation of it, varying somewhat, because of the changes that have taken place. It also gives greater prominence to Home Missions.

Early in the decade of years, over which this History extends, some of our Presbyterian brethren separated themselves from us and united with others who had just come to Wisconsin, in establishing churches in connection with the New School General Assembly, retaining, however, their former relation to the American Home Missionary

Society. Since that movement was commenced, both ministers and churches have, in a few instances, changed their ecclesiastical relations, some in one direction and some in the other, and it is deemed almost essential to the integrity of this history, especially as it relates to Home Missions, that the ministers and churches constituting the Synod of Wisconsin, should be included. But having had no opportunity to consult them so as to secure their co-operation as a Synod, it is thought best that so much of the history as relates to them should be placed in an Appendix.

Some have expressed a wish to have the former history re-published. To meet that wish, in past at least, the most important portions of that work are brought forward in this.

Various causes have existed for the delay in getting this little volume ready for distribution, principally the claims of other duties and the labor required in its preparation.

Perfect accuracy of statements and statistics is not claimed; much care, however, has been taken to give a true history—one that will interest and benefit the people of God, and furnish cause of gratitude for what he has done.

COMMITTEE OF THE CONVENTION:

M. P. KINNEY, Stated Clerk of Beloit Convention,
A. CLARKE, " " Milwaukee "
S. W. EATON, " " Min'al Point "
H. M. PARMALEE, " " Madison "
I. N. CUNDALL, " " Winnebago "
M. WELLS, " " Lemonweir "
J. C. SHERWIN, " " La Crosse "
A. L. CHAPIN, President of Beloit College,
N. D. GRAVES, Pastor 2d Congregational Church, Beloit.

CONTENTS.

PART I.

CONTENTS.

PART II.

HISTORY OF MINISTERS.

HISTORY OF CHURCHES.

PART III.

HOME MISSIONS.

CONTENTS.

Corrections.

The name of H. Avery, on page 72, should be in the next table, on page 73.

The age of	A. Montgomery,	deceased, on p. 80,	should be	51
"	J. O. Knapp,	"	" "	41
"	O. S. Powell,	"	" "	44
"	D. W. Pickard,	"	" "	30
"	Mr. Steele,	"	"	unknown.

The names of D. Lamb and N. Miller, on page 72, should have been erased. They died while this book was being printed. Their names were placed with others who had died, and are on the same page, 80. There was not time to obtain their ages.

Efforts were made to obtain statistics of others, but without success.

A summary statement of the number of ministers was intended, like that of churches and houses of worship; also of church members. They are as follows:

Ministers now in the State	169
Ministers who have labored here and left since 1850	70
Ministers who have labored here since 1850, and have died, some here and some away	20
Whole number of deaths previous to 1850	10
Church members in 1850, and of the churches organized since, at the time of their organization	5,714
Members 1st January, 1861	10,145
Increase in 10 years, besides deaths, dismissions and removals	4,431

Other corrections and additions might be made. Those concerned will please bear in mind, that the Author has had other duties constantly claiming attention, and enough to occupy his whole time; that making books has been no part of the work of his life; that books composed largely of statistics are probably the most difficult to make; and then please do him the favor to believe that he has honestly and earnestly aimed to do justice to them and to the work in hand. With confidence in the charity and forbearance of his brethren, it is committed to them and to the churches, hoping that it will do good and not hurt, and like that of his Predecessor, bear witness to the goodness and grace of God our Savior, when he is no more.

PART I.

HISTORY OF THE GENERAL AND DISTRICT CONVENTIONS.

Organization of the General Convention.

THE first Ecclesiastical Body was a Presbytery, which was organized at Milwaukee, Jan. 17, 1839, and was called the Presbytery of Wisconsin. It consisted of four ministers and two delegates; viz.: Revs. Gilbert Crawford, Lemuel Hall, Moses Ordway and Cyrus Nichols, and Elder Samuel Hinman, of the Presbyterian church of Milwaukee, and Deacon Asa Clarke, of the Congregational church of Prairieville (now Waukesha). The Presbytery was never connected with a Synod or General Assembly.

At a meeting, July 5th, the same year, the name was changed to the Presbytery of Milwaukee, and other members were received. Other meetings were held, and other ministers and churches were received; and in October, 1840, a special meeting was held at Troy, and at the same time and place, a meeting of Congregational ministers and delegates was held, both having in view a Plan of Union, which should unite all the ministers and churches in Wisconsin, of those two denominations. After consultation and much prayer by the members of both bodies, the Union was agreed upon, and the General Convention of Wisconsin was organized.

The members composing it were as follows:

MINISTERS.

Rev. David A. Sherman, of East Troy.
" Lemuel Hall, of Geneva.
" Moses Ordway, of South Prairieville.
" Jeremiah Porter, of Green Bay. (Omitted by mistake in the former history.)
" Stephen Peet, of Milwaukee.
" Otis F. Curtis, of Prairieville (now Waukesha.)
" Cyrus Nichols, of Spring Prairie.
" Solomon Chaffee, of Platteville.
" J. U. Parsons, without charge.

CHURCHES.

There were delegates from sixteen churches, eight Presbyterian and eight Congregational, as follows: Milwaukee, Green Bay, Geneva, Racine, Whitewater, East Troy, South Prairieville, Platteville, Kenosha, Beloit, Waukesha, Milton, Salem, Troy, Caldwell's Prairie and Lisbon.

Permanency of the Arrangement.

When this Union was agreed upon, the idea of separate organizations was abandoned, and the Convention was regarded by all concerned as a permanent arrangement. See History of Churches in Wis., p. 30.

After ten or twelve years, when the spirit of denominationalism began to be agitated by some in the ministry and churches at the East and the West, the General Convention in session at Madison, in October, 1853, appointed a committee to prepare a paper setting forth, briefly, the principles of our organization, and the reasons for its continuance.

That committee reported the following, which was adopted. See 1st page of the Minutes of 1853.

Plan of Organization.

"The Presbyterian and Congregational Convention of Wisconsin was formed in October, 1840. Its design was to unite the ministers and churches of these two denominations in one body, for the more effective prosecution of the missionary work. The basis of the Union is such as to allow each church to be constituted and governed according either to the Presbyterian, or to the Congregational form of Church Government, as the majority of its members may prefer. This basis is set forth in the first Article of the Constitution. "Churches belonging to this Convention may adopt either the Presbyterian or the Congregational mode of government, and shall each be represented at the meetings of the Convention, by one delegate."

Presbyterian churches connected with the Convention do not therefore give up anything essential to the Presbyterian mode of church government, neither are they required to adopt any procedure inconsistent therewith. The Book of Discipline is followed by them in all matters of government and discipline. They have their Elders, are amenable to the higher judicatory—the District Convention, with which they are connected, as to a Presbytery, and have the right of appeal to the General Convention, which sustains to them the relation of a Synod. Their want of direct connection with the General Assembly is not considered as invalidating their right to be known and acknowledged as purely Presbyterian churches.

The Congregational churches, connected with Convention, are also constituted and governed strictly upon Congregational principles. Convention claims and exercises no judicial authority over them, but is to them, in matters of government, an advisory body, or a standing council. Each Congregational church is regarded as possessing the full right to govern itself, subject only to Christ the Great Head of the Church. In matters of public importance, advice is sought by such churches from councils specially called, or from the Convention, according to good usage among Congregational churches.

Convention, therefore, is not an amalgamation of Presbyterianism and Congregationalism, but a cordial union of *brethren* of both these denominations, who, agreeing in doctrinal belief, mode of worship, and the prosecution of the same missionary work, do not consider the difference between them upon the mode of church government so great as to make it either necessary or expedient that they should walk apart. Neither is it the design of this body to build up one of these denominations to the destruction of the other, but rather to build up churches of Christ, whether they be constituted Presbyterially or Congregationally. Accordingly it desires to be looked upon, not as an enemy to either of these branches of Christ's family, but as belonging to and a part of both, and as practically exhibiting oneness which it is believed actually exists between them.

These, then, are some of the more prominent advantages of this organization :

1. It secures the union of those who, by common consent, are virtually one, and who, in their present position and circumstances, ought not to be divided.

2. It enables Presbyterians and Congregationalists to work harmoniously together in the same field. This it does by removing the occasions of strife and ill-will and fault-finding between them, which are prone to arise when they are at rivalry.

3. It prevents the division of feeble churches, and the unnecessary multiplication of churches on the same field. Nearly all our churches are composed of members connected both with Presbyterian and Congregational churches. To separate these members, is what they are not yet able to bear.

4. It is in harmony with the American Home Missionary Society, in which both Presbyterians and Congregationalists unite to carry forward the work of Home Missions. Of this Society, nearly all the churches of the Convention have been, or are, beneficiaries, and its ministers, missionaries. There is certainly reason in the union of those on the same field, who are sent out and sustained by this great and good institution.

5. It gives greater efficiency to the Home Missionary work. It does this by securing that strength which is the result of union and co-operation, and also, by leading its ministry and churches to direct their main efforts to the advancement of the Redeemer's Kingdom, while the question, whether a church shall be governed by a session, or

by the congregation of believers, is regarded of minor importance."

This historical statement and declaration of the principles of the organization, and the reasons for their approval and perpetuity, has been repeatedly in the minutes of meetings of the Convention, since 1853.

ORGANIZATION OF DISTRICT CONVENTIONS PREVIOUS TO 1850.

At a regular meeting of the General Convention, held in Geneva, in June, 1842, the District Conventions of Milwaukee, Beloit and Mineral Point were erected, their boundaries arranged, the ministers and churches were set off accordingly, and the time and place of their meetings designated.

See His. Wis. Chs., p. 13.

Milwaukee District Convention.

The boundaries assigned to this Convention were all the Lake shore counties, from the State line south to Green Bay on the north. It consisted of twelve ministers and sixteen churches, and the first meeting was held at Waukesha, June 28th, 1842.

Beloit District Convention.

The boundaries assigned to this Convention were the territory lying between the Lake counties on the east and the mining region west, and from the State line south to Lake Winnebago on the north, and it consisted of nine ministers and fifteen churches. The first meeting was held at Milton (then called Prairie du Lac), Sept. 18th, 1842.

Mineral Point District Convention.

The bounds assigned to this Convention were those which included what is termed "the mineral region." Most of the counties then organized extended to the Mississippi river. It consisted of four ministers and eleven churches, and the first meeting was held at Platteville, September 4th, 1842.

Madison District Convention.

This Convention was organized in October, 1846, and included the northern part of Beloit Convention; viz.:—the counties of Jefferson, Dane, and also Dodge, Sauk, Columbia, Marquette, Fond du Lac, Winnebago, Calumet and Brown counties. It had fifteen ministers and seventeen churches, and held the first meeting at Beaver Dam in November, 1846.

These four District Conventions were organized previous

to the date where the present history of churches begins, and for a more full account of their organization, and also of their relations to the General Convention and to the churches, see His. of Chs., p. 36, &c., by Rev. Stephen Peet.

ORGANIZATION OF DISTRICT CONVENTIONS SINCE 1851.

Winnebago District Convention

Was organized in October, 1851, and consisted of all the ministers and churches in the counties north of Columbia, Dodge and Sauk. The first meeting was held at Oshkosh in November, 1851. These counties were set off from Madison Convention. Afterwards, October, 1854, the ministers and churches in Sheboygan county and all north of it were set off to this Convention, from Milwaukee District Convention. See Minutes of 1854, p. 8.

La Crosse District Convention.

At a meeting of ministers and delegates from churches in the vicinity of La Crosse, held at Sparta, Monroe county, in June,.1855, the subject of an Ecclesiastical Organization was under consideration, according to previous consultation. There were present, Rev. J. C. Sherwin, of La Crosse, L. L. Radcliff, of Viroqua, W. Bigelow, of Black River Falls, and W. F. Avery, of Sparta, and two or three delegates. The Convention was organized at that meeting, adopted the principles and rules of other District Conventions, and voted to request to be received into the General Convention.

At the meeting of General Convention, held at Beloit in October following, the request was presented and the Convention received. The bounds assigned to it were, "the tract bounded by Wisconsin, Mississippi and St. Croix rivers, except the counties of Sauk, Richland and Crawford," and it was composed of the four ministers already named, and the churches of La Crosse, Viroqua, Sparta and Black River Falls. This territory had never been recognized by the General Convention as within its bounds, and none of the ministers or churches were in its connection. The region was but recently settled, the ministers were all home missionaries, and the churches had all been recently organized by them. Hence, previous action by General Convention, according to usage in ordinary cases, was not deemed necessary, and the organization was approved, and regarded as evidence of great progress in the work of Home Missions in that newly settled portion of the State.

Lemonwier District Convention.

At the meeting of the General Convention held at LaCrosse, in Oct., 1858, the following action which was taken gives a history of the organization, boundaries and members constituting this Convention :

ORGANIZATION OF NEW CONVENTION.

The Committee on the organization of a new Convention and the re-construction of boundary lines of Conventions, report, recommending that a new Convention be organized, consisting of all the ministers and churches located as follows:

The north half of Sauk county, the whole of Juneau, Adams, Marquette, and Waushara counties, and extending North to such limits as may hereafter be defined.

This will take from the Madison Convention five churches, viz:—Baraboo, Reedsburg, Lyndon, Newport and New Lisbon, and leave 17, as by last year's Report. It will also take the following ministers,: W. Cochran, S. Dwinnell, H. Hutchinson.

From Winnebago Convention it will take Marquette and Waushara counties, in which are six churches, viz: Green Lake, Brooklyn, Princeton, Wautoma, Leon and Richford, and leave 24: And Ministers also as follows: A. C. Lathrop, R. Everdell, H. M. Chapin, N. Miller, S. Bristol —in all 5.

Within the bounds as here described are, in all, the following churches, of which some have recently been organized and not yet reported to Conventions. Also, some Ministers who are not as yet in our Convention, but design to be.

Total Churches:—Baraboo, Reedsburg, Lyndon, Newport, New Lisbon, Mauston, Necedah, Quincy, Rochearee, N. Chester, Westfield, Wautoma, Leon, Richford, Kilbourn City, and perhaps one or two more. Total 18 churches.

And Ministers as follows:—W Cochran, H. Hutchinson,

S. Dwinnell, M. Wells, H. Hanmer, J. W. Perkins, A. C. Lathrop, R. Everdell, N. Miller. H. M. Chapin. Total, 11.

The Committee also recommend that the said ministers, and churches by their delegates, meet at Kilbourn City the last Wednesday in October, at 7 o'clock, for the purpose of organizing the new Convention. That the oldest minister present preside until a Moderator is appointed.

That, the Convention be called the Lemonwier District Convention, or by such other name as a majority present may prefer.

And that brethren Wells, Cochran and Lathrop be a Committee of arrangements for the meeting to effect such organization.

CONSTITUTIONS.

OF THE GENERAL CONVENTION.

ARTICLE I.

This Convention shall consist of the ministers and a delegate from each church belonging to the District Conventions in the State of Wisconsin; and shall adopt the fundamental principle contained in the first article of their Constitution, as the basis of its organizrtion.

ARTICLE II.

The Convention shall meet at least once in each year, and shall be opened with a sermon by the last moderator, and all its sessions shall be opened and closed with prayer.

ARTICLE III.

A moderator and temporary Clerk shall be chosen annually. The Convention shall also have a stated clerk and treasurer, which offices may be held by the same person.

ARTICLE IV.

This Convention shall receive and act on all appeals and references which may be brought regularly before them, and shall give their advice and instruction in all cases submitted to them. They shall erect District Conventions, and review their records; shall constitute the highest court of appeal, and the bond of union, peace and mutual confidence among our churches; and shall take measures for the promotion of the benevolent objects of the day.

ARTICLE V.

In all cases of trial in a District Convention, the evidence on both sides shall be fairly taken and recorded; and in cases of appeal, this evidence shall be presented to this Convention as the ground of their decision.

ARTICLE VI.

Any five ministers, belonging to the Convention, and as many delegates as may be present, being met at the time and place appointed, shall be a quorum competent to do business.

ARTICLE VII.

At the meeting of the Convention, an account shall be given of the state of religion within its bounds, and a committee shall be appointed to prepare a narrative for publication.

ARTICLE VIII.

Each District Convention shall annually send up their records to this body for examination, together with a statistical report.

ARTICLE IX.

Considering the importance of harmony in the Christian Church, and the duty of all its ministers and members to unite in promoting the interests of the Redeemer's Kingdom, and sympathizing more particularly with our brethren of the Presbyterian and Congregational churches in the United States, this Convention will hold correspondence with their general ecclesiastical bodies by delegation or otherwise, as far as may be practicable.

ARTICLE X.

Delegates from corresponding bodies shall be entitled to deliberate and advise, but not to vote in any decisions of the Convention.

ARTICLE XI.

All amendments or alterations of this Constitution or of the Confession of Faith shall require the concurrence of a majority of the Discrict Conventions, and no amendment of their Constitution or of the Confession of Faith shall be adopted until it shall have been submitted to this body and received its sanction.

OF THE DISTRICT CONVENTIONS.

ARTICLE I.

Churches belonging to this Convention, may adopt either the Presbyterian or Congregational mode of Government, and shall each be represented at the meeting of the Convention by one Delegate.

As this article constitutes the basis of this organization, it shall never be altered except by the consent of all the churches connected with the Convention.

ARTICLE II.

This Convention shall hold an annual and semi-annual meeting; and each meeting shall be opened with a sermon by the last moderator, and all its sessions shall be opened and closed with prayer.

ARTICLE III.

A moderator and temporary clerk shall be chosen at each stated meeting; and at the annual meeting, a treasurer and standing committee shall be chosen, who shall hold their office until others are appointed. The Convention shall also have a stated clerk.

ARTICLE IV.

A committee shall also be appointed at the annual meeting, to conduct the several parts of the examination of candidates who may apply to this body for licensure or ordination.

ARTICLE V.

The moderator shall, on the application of two ministers and one church, call a special meeting of the Convention, specifying in his letters of notification, the particular business for which the meeting is called; and no other business shall be finally decided at that meeting. These letters of notification shall be communicated to each minister and church connected with this body, at least ten days before the time appointed for the meeting of Convention.

ARTICLE VI.

It shall be the duty of the stated clerk, besides recording the transactions of the Convention, to preserve the records carefully, and to grant extracts from them; and such extracts, or any certificates, under the hand of the stated clerk, shall be considered as authentic vouchers of the fact which they declare.

ARTICLE VII.

The standing committee shall consist of not less than four ministers, whose duty it shall be to examine the credentials of ministers and licentiates, who may wish the approbation of this body, during its recess; and on receiving satisfaction respecting their good standing and qualification to preach the gospel, they shall recommend them to the churches.

ARTICLE VIII.

Licentiates, under the care of this Convention, shall be amenable to it for their preaching and moral conduct, yet not so as to interfere with the prerogative of the church, to which the licentiate belongs, to exercise discipline over him.

ARTICLE IX.

When any minister proposes to join this Convention, it shall be the duty of the Convention to satisfy themselves respecting his religious sentiments and conduct, and reject or admit him as they shall deem expedient. The Convention shall also satisfy themselves respecting the religious sentiments and christian practice of any church, before admitting it to this body.

ARTICLE X.

Every minister connected with this Convention who shall organize a church within its bounds, shall instruct those wishing to be so organized respecting the regulations of this body, and urge them to connect themselves with this Convention, and shall report the same at the next meeting.

ARTICLE XI.

Churches which adopt the Presbyterian form of government may elect their Ruling Elders either for a limited period or for life.

ARTICLE XII.

Appeals, complaints, protests, &c., may come up to the Convention from Congregational churches, in the same manner as from those that are Presbyterian; or, the decision of the church shall be finpl, as shall be fixed upon by a standing rule of the church.

ARTICLE XIII.

In case of an appeal from a lower judicatory, the action of this body shall be final; but any judical process originating in this body may be carried by complaint or appeal to the General Convention.

ARTICLE XIV.

In all cases of trial in a lower judicatory, the evidence on both sides shall be fairly taken and recorded, and in cases of appeal, this evidence shall be presented to this Convention as the ground of their decision.

ARTICLE XV.

Each church shall exhibit their records to the Convention once a year for examination, and shall present a statistical report at the annual meeting.

ARTICLE XVI.

At each stated meeting of the Convention, an account shall be given of the state of religion within our bounds, and a committee shall be appointed to prepare a narrative.

ARTICLE XVII.

The Convention will ordinarily celebrate the Lord's supper at their annual meeting.

ARTICLE XVIII.

This Convention shall receive and act on all appeals and references which may be regularly brought before them, and shall give their advice and instruction in all cases submitted to them.

ARTICLE XIX.

Any three ministers and as many delegates as may be present, belonging to the Convention, being met at the time and place appointed, shall be a quorum, competent to do business.

ARTICLE XX.

Ministers in good standing in other ecclesiastical bodies who may be present, may be invited to sit with the Convention as corresponding members. They shall be entitled to deliberate and advise, but not to vote in any decisions of the Convention.

ARTICLE XXI.

All amendments or alterations of this constitution shall be submitted to the General Convention, agreeably to the provisions of their constitution on the subject.

RULES OF BUSINESS.

1. The moderator shall call the Convention to order at the hour to which it stands adjourned; and, on the appearance of a quorum, shall open the meeting with prayer.

2. If a quorum be not assembled at the hour appointed, any two members shall be competent to adjourn from time to time, that an opportunity may be given for a quorum to assemble

3. After calling the roll, the minutes of the last sitting shall be read, and, if necessary, corrected.

4. Immediately after the opening of each meeting of the Convention a committee of business shall be appointed; and, in ordinary cases, no business, unless it be some of the usual routine, shall be taken up, until it be regularly presented by this committee.

5. When the moderator shall call to order, each member shall take his seat, and give due attention to business—avoiding all unnecessary walking, talking, whispering, and every thing inconsistent with good order.

6. The members shall be particular in attending at the stated hours; and no member shall absent himself during the session, without the moderator's leave, nor withdraw entirely, without leave of the Convention.

7. The moderator may speak on points of order, in preferrence to other members, rising from his seat; and shall decide questions of order, subject, however, to an appeal to the Convention; but he shall not take part in the usual debates, unless he places some other person in the chair.

8. Before debate on any subject, a motion must be made and seconded, and afterwards repeated by the moderator; and every motion shall be reduced to writing, if the moderator or any other member require it.

9. Any member having made a motion, shall have liberty to withdraw it before any debate is had thereon; but not afterwards, without permission from the Convention.

10. On questions of order, adjournment, or commitment, no person shall speak more than once, and on other questions, no member shall speak more than twice, without leave from the Convention.

11. When a question is under debate, no motion shall be received, unless to amend, to commit, to postpone, or to adjourn.

12. An amendment may be made on any motion, and shall be decided before the original motion.

13. If any question under debate, contains several parts, any member may have it divided, and a vote taken on each part.

14. A question shall not be re-considered at the same meeting of the Convention at which it was decided, without the concurrence of two thirds of the members who were present at that decision; nor unless the motion for re-consideration be made and seconded by members who voted in the majority.

15. Every member, in speaking, shall address himself to the moderator, shall treat his fellow-members with respect, and shall not indulge in personal reflections.

16. If any member act in any respect in a disorderly manner, it shall be the duty of the moderator, and the privilege of any member, to call him to order.

17. No speaker shall be interrupted, unless he be out of order, or for the purpose of correcting mistakes or misrepresentations.

18. If two or more members rise at the same time to speak, the one most distant from the moderator's chair, shall speak first.

19. Any member who may think himself injured by any decesion of the Convention, may have his dissent, or protest, with his reasons, entered on the records, or put on the file, if given in before the Convention rise, and if expressed in decent and respectful language.

20. The clerk shall record, as minutes of the Convention, all business that comes regularly before them, and all final decisions of such business, unless otherwise directed by the Convention; and at the close of the session, the clerk shall read the whole of the minutes, that they may be reviewed in connection, and corrected, if necessary, by the Convention, previous to their adjournment.

21. It is the duty of the moderator to appoint all committees, except in those cases in which the Convention shall decide otherwise.

22. The person first named on any committee, shall be considered as the chairman thereof, whose duty it shall be to convene the committee; and in case of his absence, or inability to act, the second named member shall take his place, and perform his duties.

23. When various motions are made with respect to the filling of blanks with particular numbers or times, the question shall always be first taken on the highest number, and the longest time.

24. When the moderator has commenced taking the vote, no further debate or remark shall be admitted, unless there has evidently been a mistake; in which case, the mistake shall be rectified, and the moderator shall re-commence taking the vote.

25. When a vote is taken by ballot, the moderator shall vote with the other members; but he shall not vote in any other case, unless the Convention be equally divided; when, if he do not choose to vote, the question shall be lost.

26. The yeas and nays on any question shall not be recorded, unless it be required by one third of the members present.

27. The moderator of the Convention, in finally closing its sessions, in addition to prayer, may cause a hymn to be sung, and shall pronounce the apostolic benediction.

28. A suitable number of copies of these rules shall be furnished by the stated clerk, for the use of the moderator and members, during the meeting of Convention.

CONFESSION OF FAITH.

ARTICLE I.

We believe there is one God, the Creator, Preserver, and Governor of the universe; that He is a Spirit, self-existent, independent, unchangeable, eternal, infinite in being, wisdom, power, holiness, justice, goodness, mercy, and truth.

ARTICLE II.

We believe that the scriptures of the Old and New Testament were given by inspiration of God; that they contain a complete and harmonious system of divine truth; and are the only perfect rule of religious faith and practice.

ARTICLE III.

We believe that there are three persons in the God-head, the Father, the Son, and the Holy Ghost; that these three are in essence one, and in all divine perfections equal.

ARTICLE IV.

We believe that God governs all things according to His eternal and infinitely wise purpose, so as to render them condusive to His own glory, and the greatest good of the universe, and in perfect consistency with His hatred of sin, the free agency of man, and the importance of the use of means,

ARTICLE V.

We believe that man in his primitive state was perfectly holy; that he fell from that state by sinning against God; and in consequence of the apostacy of Adam, all mankind are totally depraved, and by nature children of wrath, and cannot be restored to the favor of God without an atonement.

ARTICLE VI.

We believe that the Lord Jesus Christ, the only and well beloved Son of God, assumed our nature, perfectly obeyed the law of God, suffered and died, the just for the unjust, making a sufficient atonement for the sins of all mankind; that God can now consistently exercise mercy towards sinners, and that He will pardon all those who repent and believe the gospel.

ARTICLE VII.

We believe that God did from eternity choose some of the human race to salvation through sanctification of the Spirit and belief of the truth; and that all those whom He has thus chosen, He will renew and sanctify in this life, and keep them by His power, through faith unto salvation.

ARTICLE VIII.

We believe that in order to acceptance with God, the sinner must be born again, and that regeneration is a moral change produced by the influence of the Holy Spirit operating on the mind through the truth.

ARTICLE IX.

We believe that men are free and voluntary in all their conduct; that their entire depravity, the purpose of God respecting their salvation, and the agency of the spirit in regeneration, do not destroy or in the least impair their free agency; that the offer of salvation is freely and sincerely made to all men; and that those who perish under the light of the gospel, perish by voluntarily rejecting its offers of eternal life.

ARTICLE X.

We believe that Christians are justified freely by grace through faith; and that although they are thus freely justified, still the law of God as a rule of duty remains in full force; and that all men are under obligations perfectly to obey it.

ARTICLE XI.

We believe that the visible church of Christ consists of professing Christians who publicly profess their faith in him, and covenant to walk together in the ordinances of the gospel.

ARTICLE XII.

We believe in the divine appointment of the Christain Sabbath, and of the Sacraments of the New Testament, Baptism, and the Lord's Supper, which all are under obligation in the exercise of faith to observe; and that it is the duty of parents to dedicate their children to God in baptism and train them up in the nurture and admonition of the Lord.

ARTICLE XIII.

We believe that the soul is immortal, and that the last day Christ will raise the dead and judge the world in righteousness; that all who die impenitent will go away into everlasting punishment; and the righteous be received to heaven to enjoy eternal felicity.

COVENANT.

You, viewing yourselves subjects of special divine grace, and under obligation to confess Christ before men, do now, in the presence of God, angels, and men, acknowledge your obligations to be the Lord's, and do here solemnly consecrate yourselves and all you have, forever, to God, through Jesus

Christ. You renounce the ways of sin, and choose the Lord Jehovah to be your God and eternal portion; the Lord Jesus Christ to be your only Savior, and the Holy Ghost to be your Sanctifier and Comforter. You take God's Holy Word to be your rule of faith and practice, and you engage by the help of his grace to conform to it in all your conduct. You promise to maintain and constantly attend all the institutions and ordinances of the gospel, baptism and the Lord's supper, public worship, and the strict observance of God's holy Sabbath.

You promise daily to maintain secret prayer, to encourage family worship and the seasonable dedication of children to God in baptism, and to instruct, govern and restrain from vicious practices and company all who may be under your care. You promise not to conform to the world or indulge in vain conversation or amusement, and totally to abstain from the use and traffic of all intoxicating drinks as a beverage. You promise to promote the edification, purity and peace of the Church, to watch over its members in Christian meekness and brotherly love, and to submit to its discipline until you are regularly dismissed therefrom, endeavoring in all things to walk worthy of the vocation wherewith you are called. Relying on divine grace, thus you covenant with God and this church.

RESPONSE OF THE CHURCH.

We, then, the members of this church, do cordially receive you into our communion and fellowship. We welcome you as members of the body of Christ, and as fellow travellers to His rest. We promise by the grace of God to watch over you with meekness and love, and by council and prayer to help you forward in the way to Heaven. And may we live together as brethren, glorify Him on earth, and finally join the church triumphant in heaven, there to unite in the praises of God and the Lamb. Amen.

POWERS AND RELATIONS OF THE CONVENTIONS.

"The great principle involved in this arrangement is contained in the first article of the constitution, which is fundamental and unalterable, as follows:

Churches belonging to this Convention may adopt either the Presbyterian or the Congregational mode of government, and shall each be represented at the meetings of the Convention by one delegate.

In the organization of a church, the form of government is decided by the vote of the majority of the members, and the church acts and is governed accordingly. The minority yield their preferences and coincide with the form of government thus adopted. There is no amalgamation or mixture of the two modes of government in the same church. The difficulty of this complex arrangement is wholly avoided, except perhaps in one or two instances. Each church is either Presbyterian or Congregational, and transacts its business according to the established rules and usages of other churches of the same order. Presbyterians and Congregationalists agree to unite and act in one body on these principles, regarding themselves as brethren of the same faith, and recognizing the right of the majority to decide in matters of this kind."

Relations of the Convention to Presbyterian Churches.

"The Convention sustains the same relation to Presbyterian churches connected with it as a Presbytery, and has the same jurisdiction over them. The churches, by their adoption of the Presbyterian mode of government, impliedly agree to be governed by the principles and rules of Presbyterian bodies. They transact their business according to the Book of Discipline of the Presbyterian church of the United States, and have the right of appeal. The only modification is in regard to the election of elders for a limited time, or for life. Most of the churches elect for a limited period, generally for one, two or three years, and at the expiration of that time elect others or re-elect the same. This provision was made by the Presbytery of Wisconsin while under the constitution of the Presbyterian church in the United States, and was thence incorporated into the constitution of the Convention."

Relations of the Convention to Congregational Churches.

"The Congregational churches in Wisconsin are purely Congregational, and retain all their rights and privileges as such. They do their business in a congregational way, and the decision of the church is final. The Convention stands in the same relation to Congregational churches as an Association, with lay delegation, or rather a *con-sociation.* It has, however, no jurisdiction over the churches, unless, by the action of the church, appeals are allowed, or cases are referred to Convention for decision."

"There is a provision in the Constitution which requires the records of the churches to be reviewed; but this rule does not give the Convention any *control* in a judicial sense. It is designed, so far as Congregational churches are concerned, to afford opportunity for advice and suggestion in regard to the manner of keeping records, and to enable Convention to discover any essential disorders or departure from sound doctrine, in which case they have the right to withdraw fellowship from the church, aud thus dissolve the connection."

Relation of the Convention to Ministers.

"Ministers connected with the Conventions are governed by the constitution, or rules of business, as far as they may specify. The constitution, however, makes no provision for discipline, but purposely leaves it to the rules and usages of the denominations concerned. Hence in case of the discipline of a minister, the Convention follows the rules and usages of the denomination which he prefers. The trial of a Congregational minister is conducted as such trials are conducted in Congregational bodies in New England or elsewhere.

In case of a Presbyterian minister, the trial is conducted according to the Book of Discipline in the same manner as in a Presbytery. He has, however, only one appeal, viz., from the District Convention to the General Convention.

Councils.

"Congregational churches are at liberty to call councils, if they choose. Councils have been held, at various times, from an early period, and for all the purposes for which councils are called, namely, the ordination, installation and dismission of ministers, and for organizing churches; and the Convention has given its sanction, by the admission of ministers so ordained and the churches so organized. Most business of this kind is, however, transacted by the District Conventions, as a matter of convenience, and is the preference of the churches."

See His. of Chs. in Wis., p. 36.

These powers and relations of the Conventions to each other, to the ministers and the churches, were elementary principles, adopted at the organization of the General Convention.

Their practical working, the past twenty years, may be seen in the results.

The past ten years have been years of denominational agitation throughout the land. Outside influences have not been wanting, to produce a rupture here, and a separation. Ministers and churches composing this body have not been indifferent witnesses of these agitations, and their meetings have been open to the free discussion of questions of difference affecting the two denominations.

Every church and every man in this connection claims

and concedes the right of denominational preference, and the time may come when the example furnished by others will be followed by us, and "Abraham and Lot" go apart here as elsewhere.

But experience thus far, and the claims of the great interests of our common Christianity in this region, do not furnish considerations in favor of separation, but of continued co-operation.

Doctrinal Views.

"The doctrinal views of the ministers and churches may be seen in their Confession of Faith. Measures were taken at an early period to provide a well expressed and sound Confession of Faith and Covenant. The one in use among us was prepared with great care by a committee, and after mature consideration was unanimously adopted by the Convention as an expression of their doctrinal sentiments, and recommended to be used by the churches. It is made the duty of the Conventions, by their constitution, when a minister proposes to unite with the body, to "satisfy themselves respecting his religious sentiment and conduct." All who have been received into the Convention have given their cordial assent to this Confession of Faith, and it is believed that they hold and preach those great doctrines of the Reformation which are held by the ecclesiastical bodies with which we are in correspondence.

"The churches are not required to adopt this Confession, in *form*, but they are required to give evidence that they receive the doctrines it contains. If different articles are adopted, they are presented and examined when application for admission is made.

This Confession of Faith was printed at an early day, and has been re-printed a few years since. It is extensively circulated and adopted by most of the churches in the State, thus producing a general uniformity in this respect."

Character of the Churches.

"The religious institutions of Wisconsin, bear, in a good degree, the impress of New England. A large proportion of the population either came directly from that section of country, or are of New England descent. Our ministers are mostly all of eastern origin and eastern education. The doctrines which have made that section of country lovely and renowned, and given it such power and influence in the land, are the doctrines received by our churches, adopted by our Conventions, and preached by our ministers. To a great extent, also, the order which characterizes the churches in that region prevails among us. Our churches have been graciously preserved from the errors, disorders, and divisions which have afflicted some portions of Zion."

See His. of Chs. in Wis., in 1850, p. 187.

The foregoing statements of doctrinal views, and the character of the churches given in the history already referred to, are believed to be as applicable now as they were when first made. The additions made to the number of ministers and of churches in this connection, have been made on the basis of these doctrinal views and these characteristics.

The increase of light, and the many overturnings, peculiar to this age of reforms and of progress, have given strength, instead of weakness, to the convictions in favor of these views and characteristics. And it is entirely within the truth to say that the ministers and churches of this Convention, in respect to their belief in, and earnest maintenance of sound Christian doctrine, will not suffer by comparison with the same number of ministers and churches of any denomination.

This individual testimony is most cheerfully given, on these points, and without solicitation; and it is deemed not inappropriate in this connection, or uncalled for in giving a faithful history of churches in Wisconsin.

Table

Of the Meetings of the General Convention since 1850, showing the Place, Time, Members and Officers of each Meeting.

Place of Meeting.	Time.	Mem's Present.				Moderators.
		Min's.	Del.	Cor. mem	Del. For. Bod.	
Plattville...	Oct. 2, 1851	29	10	11	4	Rev. M. Montague.
Racine.....	" 7, 1852	54	30	9	3	" S. Peet.
Madison....	" 20, 1853	48	20	16	2	" M. P. Kinney.
Fond du Lac	" 7, 1854	41	22	13	4	" S. W. Eaton.
Beloit......	" 4, 1855	56	25	16	3	" H. Foote.
Milwaukee..	" 2, 1856	61	32	18	6	" C. W. Camp.
Oshkosh ...	" 1, 1857	42	10	9	5	" C. Boynton.
LaCrosse...	" 7, 1858	50	27	9	6	" N. D. Graves.
Janesville ..	" 2, 1859	62	25	16	7	" J. C. Sherwin.
Beaver Dam	" 4, 1860	52	20	10	6	" L. Clapp.

Character of the Meetings of General Convention.

These general gatherings of ministers, delegates, and others who love the ways of Zion, have been deeply interesting and profitable.

A general rule of rotation among the District Conventions, has been observed in holding them, so far as was practicable, so that a greater number might, in the course of years, have the benefit of them.

This fact of rotation, as to the places of meeting, may account, in part at least, for the different number of members in attendance at different times.

A leading object of the meetings being ecclesiastical in its character, more or less time has necessarily been occupied with duties in that direction.

Great prominence, however, has been given to devotional exercises, and to the consideration of objects of benevolence and subjects of reform. The presence of Delegates from foreign bodies has added much to the interest of the meetings, and not unfrequently have missionaries from foreign lands been present, and added greatly to the inspiration of the occasions.

Great unanimity has usually characterized the doings of those meetings, and although the Convention is composed of two denominations, as its name indicates, and for the past ten years those denominations over our land have been painfully agitated with questions of difference, those agitations have seldom affected our meetings.

In the midst of commotion in the denominational elements around, it has been a cause for gladness in many hearts, that we have been enabled to go quietly on with our work on the great and time honored principle of co-operation. To the working of this principle it is believed that this Convention, and the Churches in its connection, are largely indebted, under God, for the prosperity which has been and still is enjoyed.

Action on Various Subjects by the General Convention.

The position and views of the Convention in regard to benevolent efforts, reforms, and other topics will be seen from the action of the body on these subjects from time to time. Numerous resolutions, in various forms, have been discussed and adopted, and generally with entire unanimity.

Some of the resolutions passed are given in full, others have been condensed, owing to their length and to the frequency of action on the same subject; all are taken from the printed minutes, and where the precise form is not given, care has been taken to give the substance as full and definite as possible.

Nearly the same order, as to time, is observed in stating them here, as that in which they are found in the minutes.

Action on the Resignation of Rev. Stephen Peet, as Stated Clerk in 1851.

"Resolved, That we have heard, with feeling of much regret, of the painful and dangerous sickness with which it has pleased Almighty God to afflict our beloved brother and fellow laborer, Rev. Stephen Peet. We would hereby express to him our sincere sympathy in the midst of his sufferings, and our unfeigned satisfaction at the prospect of his final recovery and restoration to usefulness. We would also extend to him, in this connection, our thanks for the fidelity with which he has served this Convention for a number of years, as its stated clerk; and also express our regret that it has appeared expedient to him, at this time, to resign his office."

Mr. Peet had been the stated clerk from the organization of the Convention, in 1840. On his resignation, the Rev. Z. M. Humphrey was appointed stated clerk.

Plan for Church Erection Adopted in 1852, Page 6.

The annual meeting was held this year at Racine—Rev. S. Peet moderator.

The most important item of business was the erection of a Board of Trustees for the collection and management of a Church Erection Fund, upon the following plan, as reported by a committee:

1. There shall be appointed annually a Treasurer, a Corresponding Secretary and five Directors, who shall together constitute a Board of Trustees, who shall manage all funds contributed for the aid of feeble churches belonging to this Convention, in the erection of Houses of Worship, a majority of this Board shall constitute a quorum.

2. This Board shall be guided in the distribution of these funds by the conditions prescribed by the donors, so

far as conditions shall be affixed to any donations; and with respect to funds given unconditionally, they shall act impartially upon the basis of the Constitution of this Convention.

The officers appointed were, Rev. D. Clary, Corresponding Secretary; H. Hobart, Treasurer; Rev. A. L. Chapin, Rev. S. Peet, Rev. O. S. Powel, Rev. H. Foote, Directors.

Relative to Absent Members of Churches, 1853, Page 13.

" Whereas, in numerous instances, members of churches by removal from one place to another without applying for letters of dismission, and also by neglecting to present such letters when received, to the churches whose care they are recommended, are virtually withdrawn from all Christian fellowship, and lost to the church; it is earnestly urged upon Pastors and churches.—

1st. To exercise a more vigilant care of their members; to arrest declension as far as practicable in its incipient stages, and where necessary, to apply prompt and efficient discipline.

2d. To endeavor to impress members with a deeper sense of their obligation, in cases of removal, to transfer their church connections as soon as possible.

3d. When letters are given, to ask an official notification of the reception of members, by the churches to which they are recommended, and not to consider any member as dismissed until such notification.

4th. To use every means in their power, to gain information concerning members who have gone beyond their reach, or knowledge.

5th. In case of absent members known to be living in violation of their covenant vows, to ask the assistance of churches in whose vicinity such members reside, to carry out discipline in an orderly way.

6th. In case of persons known to be members of churches at the East, who form no church connection here, or live in violation of their covenant vows, it is recommended that after labor in accordance with the Gospel Rule, notice be given to the churches to which they formerly belonged, asking them to proceed to the necessary discipline.

The Convention believe that the faithful adoption of, and action upon these recommendations by the churches, will save some precious souls from the utter shipwreck of their faith, and deliver the visible body of Christ from many foul spots and blemishes.

In this conviction, the Convention do earnestly deprecate the practice of erasing the names of delinquent members, without the previous exercise of church discipline, or faithful effort to reach absent members."

Salaries of Ministers, 1853, Page 13.

At a meeting of the lay delegates of this Convention, called to consider the subject of ministerial support, the following resolutions were unanimously adopted, viz:

"Resolved, That in view of the increased, and increasing expensiveness of living, and cost of the means necessary for a faithful pursuit of the work of the ministry, a corresponding increase of salary is justly due to the ministers within our bounds.

"Resolved, That we invite the Convention now in session, to take such action on this subject, as may be proper to bring it to the notice of the Churches, and also to request the American Home Missionary Society, while the churches may increase their subscriptions for the support of their ministry, not to withhold its liberal and benevolent aid."

The Stockbridge Indians.

As a matter of history, it may be of interest to state that a church was organized by missionaries of the A. B. C. F. Missions in 1818, among the Indians, of that tribe at Stockbridge, Onondaga county, New York, who removed to Wisconsin in 1821, and in 1834, settled in Calumet county.

When Wisconsin, as a field of missionary labor, passed from the Foreign to the Home Mission Society, that church came into our ecclesiastical and home missionary connection. The tribe decreased in population, and the church became much embarrassed and perplexed with questions pertaining to Government and the title to their lands.

A delegate appeared before the Convention, and after a full statement of their trials and wants, the following action was taken:

"Resolved, That the present condition of the Stockbridge Indians who have a church connected with our Body, is such as to call forth our sympathy, and that we feel it incumbent upon us to endeavor to procure for them the stated ministrations of the Gospel, and that, as far as we can, individually, we will lend our aid to procure the recognition of their just rights by the General Government."

"Resolved, That a committee of five be appointed to memorialize the proper Department of the Government in our name, in behalf of the Stockbridge tribe, setting forth their grievances and petitioning for the restoration to them of their lands."

See Minutes of 1854, page 9.

The Congregational Board of Publication, 1854, p. 9.

"Resolved, That the objects of the Congregational Board of Publication, viz: "to procure and circulate such tracts and books as are adapted to explain, prove, vindicate, and illustrate the peculiar and essential doctrines of the Gospel," "with their application to duty in all the various relations of civil, social, and religious life," *Slavery not excepted*, and the circulation of Pastoral Libraries among the churches whose ministers are prohibited from purchasing books by their limited means, meet our cordial approbation, and that we recommend to our churches a hearty co-operation with the Society, not merely in the work of securing such libraries, but also by contributing to its funds.

Christian Courtesy, '54 p. 9.

"Resolved, That the principles of Christian courtesy forbid that ecclesiastical bodies and churches in fraternal correspondence should receive into their connection, churches, ministers or members, without regular letters of dismission and recommendation.

American Bible Society, '54, p. 12.

"Resolved, That the Convention retains its strong confidence in the American Bible Society, and rejoices in the evidence that it is constantly receiving marked tokens of the favor of the Lord; that we will cordially welcome its agent for this State to our churches, and aid him in securing enlarged contributions to its treasury.

Theological Seminary, '54, p. 11.

"Whereas, The subject of establishing Theological Seminaries in the North-West has for some time past been under consideration by individuals and ecclesiastical bodies; and preliminary steps have been taken towards establishing two such institutions at Chicago; and

Whereas, Such movements are of great importance to the interest of religion among us.

Resolved, That it is the opinion of this Convention that immediate and efficient measures should be taken to furnish in the North-West, Theological instructions suited to the wants of Christian young men desiring to enter the ministry.

Resolved, That in view of the numbers and condition of Theological Institutions at the East, the churches at the West cannot at present reasonably depend on the munificence of their eastern brethren, but should rely mainly on their own resources for means to provide Theological instruction for our young men.

Resolved, That in the opinion of this Convention, one Theological Institution is all that will be needed for many years to come in the North-West, for Congregationalists and N. S. Presbyterians, and that to undertake the establishment of either a distinctive Congregational or Presbyterial Seminary in the North-West, would be unwise and injurious to the best interests of Christ's Kingdom in this region.

Resolved, That we hereby declare our sincere desire for union of the two denominations in providing Theological instruction, and that we are ready to pledge our hearty co-operation in such an enterprise."

Revivals.

"Resolved, That in view of the general dearth of revivals of religion, and the manifest desirableness of more laborers in many of our churches, this Convention recommend the obtaining, if possible, the occasional assistance of approved Evangalists in such places as may desire them."

"Resolved, That we recognize with gratitude and thanksgiving the manifestation of the power and grace of God, as seen in the late wonderful religious awakenings in Ireland; and while we pray that this work may go on, we draw from it encouragement to prosecute our work in these Western regions with new zeal and hopefulness."

Assessment for Contingent Expenses.

Resolved, 1. Each church connected with the Convention shall be assessed at the rate of five cents per member; this money to be raised in such a manner as the church may elect.

2. The money thus procured, shall be collected by the Treasurers of the District Conventions, and by them transmitted to the Treasurer of the General Convention.

3. An Auditing Committee shall be appointed to audit the accounts of the Treasury.

4. The printed minutes shall be distributed, in numbers proportionate to the sums collected from the several churches.

In accordance with article 2d of this scheme, Rev. J. J. Miter and Bro. W. J. Whaling were appointed auditing committee.

Placing a Monument at the Grave of Rev. Stephen Peet.

BELOIT, Oct., 1855.

Mr. Peet came to Wisconsin in 1838. He labored in the churches at Green Bay and Milwaukee a few years, and then as Agent of the American Home Missionary Society seven years. Afterwards he was Agent of Beloit College, and then engaged in laying the foundations of the

Chicago Theological Seminary. He died in March, 1855.

Beloit had been his residence many years, and has been that of his family since his death. His remains lie in its Cemetery.

A suitable monument had been prepared, in procuring which, a great number of ministers and others in Wisconsin, Illinois and Iowa, had voluntarily participated.

The meeting of the General Convention at Beloit, in October following, was selected as a suitable time for placing the monument at his grave. Accordingly, the Convention took a recess on Saturday afternoon, Oct. 6th, and united with the citizens of Beloit, the Faculty and members of the College, and others present, and proceeded to the grave yard, and engaged in services appropriate to the occasion. Addresses were delivered by Rev. J. Porter of Green Bay, now of Chicago, and President Chapin of the College. The exercises were impressive; the monument was erected over his grave, and an appropriate record made in the minutes of the Convention. See p. 7, 1855.

Slavery.

On the evil of American Slavery, the Convention has, during the last ten years, as heretofore, calmly yet candidly and steadily, by repeated action, borne its testimony, affirming the essential antagonism of that institution to Christ's law of love, and the guilt of those who participate in it, or defend it. The following summary presents the main points referred to in resolutions passed at different times, expressed for the most part in the words of the resolutions. The Convention has said, '59, p 11 :

"1st. That we regard the voluntary claim made by one human being on another as property, as itself sin and all the adjuncts of slaveholding which involve that claim as also sinful and an abomination in the sight of God." And further, 1853, p. 15, "that the ministry and churches are bound to rebuke all sin, to labor earnestly for the removal of oppression, and to withhold Christian fellowship from all those who persist in holding in slavery their fellow men."

2d. It has expressed these convictions kindly and faithfully to the benevolent societies with which it co-operates, and other ecclesiastical bodies with which it holds correspondence. Thus it has declared the conviction, 1853, p. 6, that the American Tract Society and the American Sabbath School Union, in their attempt to furnish a Christian Literature for the country, should, though their publications, give at least the same prominence to the sin of oppression that they do to other open and flagrant sins.

With expressions of abiding interest and attachment for the American Board of Commissioners for Foreign Missions, it has respectfully urged that body, 1858, p. 12, to withdraw its support from churches where slavery still continues, and, 1854, p. 11, rejoiced in every step taken in that direction.

It has repeatedly instructed its delegates to the Presbyterian General Assembly and other bodies, to assure those to whom they have been commissioned, 1856, p. 13, that we have neither fellowship nor sympathy with those ministers and divines who hold slaves "*from principle and choice*," or who seek in the Bible, excuses and defences for the sin of American Slavery," 1854, p. 12, and to tender the ardent sympathies of the Convention to such as, standing in some ecclesiastical relation to slavery, have labored faithfully to rid themselves of the sin of slaveholding.

3d. With a spirit of true patriotism, watching the signs of the times, the Convention expresses, 1859, p. 11, sad and fearful apprehensions for our country in view of the re-opening or great increase of the slave trade between Africa and the slave states of the Union, as well as the internal slave trade among the slave states themselves, and calls on the ministers of the churches to pray and to act wherever they can against this growing iniquity.

Ministerial Education.

The Convention deeply impressed with the importance of some systematic action to encourage and sustain pious young men in a course of preparation for the Christian ministry, in the year 1858, organized a permanent committee to attend to that interest on the following plan:

The Board of Education of the Presbyterian and Congregational Convention of Wisconsin.

"1st. This Committee shall be called the Board of Education of the Presbyterian and Congregational Convention of Wisconsin.

2d. The Board shall be constituted by the election at the present meeting of two members from each District Convention, one of whom shall hold his office for one year and the other for two years. Hereafter the Convention shall annually elect one from each District Convention, who shall remain in office for two years.

3d. The Board shall organize itself immediately after its election and hereafter shall meet at least once a year, at or near the time of the annual meeting of the General Convention. It may also meet at any time by adjournment, or by special call of the Chairman, or of any three members agreeing thereto. Five members shall constitute a quorum for business.

4th. The officers of the Board shall be a Chairman, Secretary and Treasurer, to be elected by the Board from its own number. The Board shall also appoint an Executive Committee of not less than three or more than seven, located near together. The Treasurer shall be ex-officio a member of the Executive Committee, and those members of the Committee who are not members of the Board, shall be entitled to sit in deliberation with the Board, but not to vote.

5th. The Executive Committee shall be entrusted with the care and disbursement of funds contributed to the Treasury of the Board. They shall annually present to the Board a report of their proceedings, which shall be submitted to the General Convention.

6th. The Board shall adopt uniform rules for the acceptance and assistance of beneficiaries, subject always to review and modification by the Convention.

7th. The members of the Board from each Convention shall be a Committee charged with the responsibility of looking after this interest within the bounds of their own Convention. It shall be their special effort to call forth from all the churches regular contributions, to be taken, as far as practicable, on the Sabbath before the last Thursday in February, and to seek out among the churches worthy young men who may be persuaded to prepare themselves for the sacred office. They shall also be authorized to examine and recommend young men for the patronage of the Board.

8th. The Board shall also appoint in connection with those institutions in which beneficiaries may be pursuing their studies, local Committees who shall examine and recommend candidates and receive from such as are accepted their stated reports according to the uniform rules of the Board."

The Board, as now established, has its centre at Beloit, where most of the students receiving aid are in a course of study, and President Chapin is its Chairman. The following regulations have been adopted by the Board respecting Beneficiaries:

Rules for Acceptance and Aid of Beneficiaries.

"I Each applicant for aid must present to a Committee of the Board testimonials from three or more serious and respectable persons, best acquainted with him and his circumstances, stating his age, place of residence, indigence, and moral and religious character, including his church connection, talents, previous education and serious desire to devote his life to the Christian ministry. These testimonials should be sealed papers. It shall also be the duty of the Committees of the Board to satisfy themselves by personal conference of the propriety of extending aid in each case.

II. Every beneficiary shall renew his application quarterly, and at the same time forward to the Executive Committee an account of his circumstances, and his receipts and expenditures for the past quarter, together with a certificate from his instructor, to his confidence in the correctness of the report, and the propriety of renewing the appropriation.

III. The amount appropriated to each individual shall not be more than eighty dollars per annum in the preparatory, and one hundred dollars in the collegiate or theological course.

IV. Beneficiaries may at their option, subject to the discretion of the Executive Committee, receive their appropriations as gratuities; or, as loans, giving notes in the subjoined form. But all, before receiving their first appropriation, shall obligate themselves to refund what they shall have received with interest, in case of voluntary failure to enter the ministry, or of transgression of the rules of the Board. It shall, however, be in the power of the Board, at their discretion, to cancel or defer any note or obligation, when Providential circumstances shall appear to render such course proper."

Tract Operations.

Deeply impressed with the importance of furnishing the people with a sound Christian literature, the Convention has always seconded the operations of the Tract Societies on this field, and urged upon the churches the adoption of systematic tract distributien. The American Tract Society whose center of operations is in the city of New York, had the entire confidence of the churches until within a few years. But its recent course with respect to publishing on the subject of slavery has so far shaken that confidence as to call for a specific resolution of the Convention, recommending its churches to withhold contributions from the Society at New York, and contribute to the original American Tract Society, Boston, or to the American Reform Book and Tract Society at Cincinnati. The Convention is now in hearty sympathy and co-operation with the Western Tract Agency located at Chicago, which unites the interest and labors of the Boston and Cincinnati Societies.

Educational Institutions.

In the rising institutions for Christian education in this state and region, the Convention has always taken a lively interest. As it was fully represented in the counsels which originated Beloit College and Rockford Female Seminary, so has it again and again, by formal resolutions, expressed its interest, confidence and co-operation in the work of building up those institutions for the thorough Christian education of our youth. More recently Brockway College in the Northern part of the State, has also enlisted its interest and support.

With respect to theological education, the Convention, in 1854, expressed an opinion in favor of the establishment of one institution for the North-West on a broad, liberal basis, which should receive its endowment from the region and enlist the united efforts of Congregationalists and New,

School Presbyterians. The course of events since that time has rendered such a joint enterprise impracticable, and the Convention has therefore come in heartily to the recommendation and support of the Chicago Theological Seminary, now opened and in successful operation.

The Convention has also urged upon its churches the importance of fostering academies and preparatory schools and interesting themselves in the common schools of the State.

Temperance.

Upon the subject of Temperance, the Convention has held an undivided sentiment, and given, from year to year, an undivided testimony. The different stages of the reform have been successively and freely discussed and acted upon by the Convention, with a degree of unanimity that has evidenced the oneness of desire on the part of all the churches for the suppression of intemperance, and the entire removal of the evil. The Convention has given its decided approbation of the principles of the so called "Maine Law," (1853, page 11,) 1854, page 9.

For the securing of the same result, the Convention cordially welcomed the "Temperance League," and recommended to the ministers and churches its adoption as an efficient helper in the great and good work, (1854, p. 9.) and although the end is not yet, there has been no disposition to yield to discouragements or to falter in the cause. As proof of this, we have the following upon record, (1860, p. 15.)

"Resolved, That this Convention regards, with deep and *unabated* interest, the cause of temperance; that the organization of the Wis. State League and Bands of Hope, meets with our warm approbation, and that we recommend to our churches and ministers to co-operate with these organizations. Also, that we view with alarm the manufacture of domestic wines in our State, and their introduction into the domestic circle."

Home Missions.

The Convention churches have ever been cordial in their sympathy with, and support of the American Home Missionary Society. A summary of the action of Convention may be thus indicated :—

1. By an acknowledgement of a debt of gratitude to the Society to be paid by increased liberality in contributions to its funds. Min. '56, p. 12, '59, p. 13.

2. By an endeavor to bring forward and qualify young men to preach the Gospel under its patronage.

3. By a hearty approval of the action of the Society in reference to churches having slave-holding members, as also of the principle adopted by the executive committee as the basis of their action in disbursing its funds, 1857, p. 7; 1859, p. 13.

4. By an expression of unabated confidence in the fidelity and impartiality of the agents of the Society employed within our bounds, 1859, p. 13.

5. By the following unanimous expression of sentiment: "Resolved, That the work of Home Mission is eminently

the great and appropriate work of the Christian church for the west, and that a large extension of this work is of the first importance to the interest of religion and the salvation of men, 1859, p. 8.

Also, of the American Missionary Association, see Minutes of 1860, p. 10.

Doctrinal Integrity.

The question having been raised at the meeting of the General Convention in 1857, in regard to certain action by one of the District Conventions, as appeared by their records in the admission of churches in whose articles of Faith some doctrines, as maintained by the Convention, were omitted, the following was given as an expression of the views of the Convention on the subject:

"Resolved, That while we respect the feelings which have prompted the protest of Rev. Wm. F. Clarke, we reply that the essential preservation of our creed is necessary to our perpetuation and purity; and that, while we do not intend to impose upon the churches connecting themselves with us, the *language* of our Confession of Faith, we do expect the District Conventions to require of churches applying for admission, to preserve the integrity of our system of doctrine." Minutes 1857, p. 9.

Statistical Year.

Resolved, Oct., 1857, That all the District Conventions be requested to prepare their annual statistical roports from August 1st, to August 1st.

Resolution against Tobacco.

"Whereas, The use of tobacco in its various forms is injurious to the body, the mind and the moral sense, causing a waste of means which men, as stewards of God, are bound to use for good and not for evil, and tending to other evil habits. Therefore,

Resolved, That we deem the habit an immorality, and as such it should be ranked with other vices, to be avoided and opposed in all suitable ways," 1857, p. 17.

Monthly Concert.

"Resolved, That we earnestly recommend to every pastor, stated supply and church in our connection to observe the monthly concert of prayer for the Foreign Missions, to take up a collection at each concert, and also annual collection for this object after a faithful presentation of its claims."

Dancing.

"Resolved That the practice of social dancing is inconsistent with Christian character, injurious to purity, destructive to all earnest piety, at enmity with revivals of religion.

and in all cases at variance with the Pauline Rule, to 'avoid the very appearance of evil,' and not to 'cause a brother to stumble or offend,' and that we view with sorrow and corcern the fact that many professing Christians in our country encourage and indulge in it." 1860, p. 12.

The Relation of Ministers to the Ecclesiastical Bodies within whose Bounds they Labor.

"Resolved, That the Convention respectfully urges upon those members of the several District Conventions who are not residing within the bounds of their Conventions, the propriety of transferring their connection to that Convention in whose bounds they are laboring and residing."

New Plan of Church Erection.

The Board of church erection which was constituted in 1852, by reason of removals and other causes, reported at the meeting of Convention in 1858, recommending a change. The subject was under consideration in 1859, and the following plan was adopted. See minutes, p. 12.

"1. Resolved, That a committee be appointed, denominated 'The Central Committee of Church Erection,' whose duty it shall be to receive funds contributed by our churches for church erection, and forward such part of them to the Treasurer of the Congregational Union as shall not otherwise be disbursed for church erection purposes;

also, to endorse and recommend applications to the Trustees of the Congregational Union from churches needing aid to build houses of worship, and to take the general oversight of the business of church erection for this Convention.

2. That all churches in our Convention be requested to take up contributions, during one of the months assigned to the S. S. cause in our 'plan for collections,' to aid feeble churches to erect houses of worship, and the amount collected go into the fund of the Congregational Union, for that purpose, except such sums as shall be deemed necessary to aid such churches in our connection as do not come within the rules of the Union, in consideration of the action of said Union, appropriating from its funds according to their ability to aid such churches in Convention, as make application through the Committee and with their approval.

3. That a committee of one minister in each District Convention be appointed, whose duty it shall be to endeavor to secure collections from all the churches, for the purpose of church erection, and forward the amount to the Central Committee.

4. That all churches needing aid to build houses of worship, be requested to seek it through the Central Committee, instead of going to the churches at the East to obtain it.

5. That the Central Committee report to this Convention, at the next meeting' a full statement of their doings.

Relative to the Death of Ministers.

" Resolved, That it be made the duty of the stated clerk to report, hereafter, at each regular meeting of this Convention, a list of the names of members who have died during the year preceeding, with a brief biographical notice of each one, for insertion in the minutes."

Lay Labor.

This subject has been under consideration both by the Convention and the churches, and much interest has been manifested in the developement of talent and influence among lay men as auxiliary to the ministry. In 1860 the following resolutions were adopted. See minutes, p. 13.

" Whereas, It appears from statements made to this Convention, that there are many destitute settlements and neighborhoods within our bounds, and in the vicinity of churches occupied by our Ministers, where Christian influence is much needed, and might be exerted with hope of success, and which it is impracticable at present to supply with ministers.

Resolved, That the ministers of this Convention be requested to acquaint themselves, as far as possible, with the destitutions and wants around them, and to seek out such laymen as themselves and their respective churches may deem of suitable qualifications, and encourage them to go into those destitutions to hold meetings for religious purposes; in other words, to engage in lay-preaching, under the general supervision of their brethren, and with their co-operation, and report the results of these labors from time to time, to their respective Conventions.

Corresponding Bodies.

The spirit of union and co-operation which led the ministers and churches to unite at the beginning in the Conventional arrangement has grown with their growth, and has developed itself in seeking and readily accepting proposals for fraternal correspondence with other evangelical denominations. Accordingly the Convention has appointed delegates, frem year to year, to other bodies, and gladly welcomed delegates from them whenever they have visited us. The following is a list of the names of ecclesiastical bodies with which this Convention is in correspondence:

The General Conference of Maine,
" General Association of New Hampshire,
" General Association of Massachusetts,
" General Association of Connecticut,
" General Convention of Vermont,
" Rhode Island Evangelical Association,
" General Assembly of New School Presbyterians,
" New York General Association,
" Ohio General Conference,
" Michigan General Association,
" Illinois General Association,
" Iowa General Association,
" Minnesota General Conference,
" Kansas General Association,
" Oregon General Association,
" Canada Congregational Union,
" Frankean Evangelical Lutheran Synod,
" Wisconsin Presbyterian Synod, (N. S.)
" Wisconsin Baptist State Association.

The Wisconsin Methodist Episcopal Conference,
" West Wisconsin Methodist Episcopal Conference,
" North-West Wis. Methodist Episcopal Conference.

And in order to secure a delegation to a greater number of these corresponding bodies, the Convention passed the following rules:

See Minutes of 1860, p. 22.

Standing Rules.

1. Any delegate to any of the bodies with which we are in correspondence, is authorized to attend the meeting of any other of the bodies, as delegate; *provided*, neither of the regular appointees is present.

2. It shall be the duty of each person appointed principal delegate to any such body, in case he cannot attend, to give timely notice to his alternate; and in case of the inability of the alternate to attend, it shall be *his* duty to convey the fraternal salutations of this body by letter.

3. The printed minutes, containing the name and the appointment of any delegate, constitute his credentials.

4. To meet the current expenses of the Convention, the following scheme has been adopted:

(1) Each church connected with the Convention shall be annually assessed at the rate of *three* cents per member —this money to be raised in such a manner as the church may elect.

(2) The money thus procured shall be collected by the Treasurers of the District Conventions, and by them transmitted to the Treasurer of the General Convention.

(3.) The published minutes are distributed to the churches, through the Post Office, in quantities proportionate to the sums contributed by each. Churches contributing nothing are entitled to no copies of the minutes.

Particular attention is requested to the last two regulations.

Systematic Benevolence.

A PLAN FOR COLLECTIONS IN WISCONSIN.

COUNTIES.	January and February	March and April.	May and June.	July and August.	Septem'r and October.	Novemb'r and Decemb'r
Kenosha, Racine, Walworth, Waukesha, Milwaukee, Jefferson, Dodge, Washington,	Home Missions.	Educati'n	Tracts and Colpor'ge	S. Schools and Ch. Erection.	Bible Cause.	Foreign Missions.
Rock, Green, Dane. Columbia, Sauk.	Foreign Missions.	Home Missions.	Educati'n	Tracts and Colpor'ge	S. Schools and Ch. Erection.	Bible Cause.
Lafayette, Grant, Iowa, Crawford, Richland, Bad Axe.	Bible Cause.	Foreign Missions.	Home Missions.	Educati'n	Tracts and Colpor'ge	S. Schools and Ch. Erection.
Marquette, Adams Juneau, Wood, Waushara, Waupacca, Portage, Marathon,	S. Schools and Ch. Erection.	Bible Cause.	Foreign Missions.	Home Missions.	Educati'n	Tracts and Colpor'ge
Sheboygan, Fond du Lac, Winnebago, Calumet, Manitowoc, Brown Outagamie.	Tracts and Colpor'ge	S. Schools and Ch. Erection.	Bible Cause.	Foreign Missions.	Home Missions.	Educati'n
La Crosse, Monroe and all North to the State Line.	Educati'n	Tracts and Colpor'ge	S. School and Ch. Erection.	Bible Cause.	Foreign Missions.	Home Missions.

REASONS AND EXPLANATIONS.

1. This plan is the result of considerable consultation and labor, with aid from the experience of churches at the East.

2. It will tend to secure annual contributions from all the churches to all these objects of benevolence.

3. It will make the calls on the churches regular, and at proper intervals.

4. It will promote systematic, efficient and harmonious action among Agents.

5. It will aid ministers in their efforts to promote benevolence among their people, diminish the necessity for Agents in that work, and advance the cause in general.

6. This plan leaves the churches to choose their own channels for their contributions, and at liberty to contribute to other objects whose claims may be presented, at least occasionally, to their consideration.

PART II.

HISTORY OF MINISTERS.

Explanation.

The following tabular form of the history of ministers, is adopted, instead of one more extended, as in the former history, for the following reasuns :

1st. The number of Ministers is now so great that it would make this book quite too large and expensive if even a brief sketch of the history of each were given.

2d. Wisconsin, as a field of ministerial and home missionary labor, is better known than when the former history was written, and the leading facts here given are deemed sufficient to answer the design of this work, and to give the necessary information on this point.

The names of ministers who were in Wisconsin in 1850, and are still here, are placed by themselves, and first in order, and then follow the names of those who have come to the State since 1850, and are still here. This arrangement gives at one view, the names of all who are now in Wisconsin, and their present fields of labor, &c.

This, however, does not include those who, in 1850, were members of the Convention, and have connected themselves with the Synod, nor those Welch ministers who belong to Convention. Both will be found in their connections.

A like arrangement will be seen in the table of the names of those ministers who have left the State, and those who have died. A few names are included in these tables of those who are not in fact members of the Convention, but whose labors are in its churches, or whose sympathies and purposes are understood to be in that direction, with perhaps one or two exceptions.

The work of Home Missions in Wisconsin being a prominent object of this history, less care has been taken to be exact in giving a statement of ecclesiastical relations, yet, about the same measure of accuracy in this respect, obtains in this, as in the former history.

If omissions and inaccuracies of dates, names, &c., are detected, those concerned may be assured that they are not the result of a want of much labor and care.

To put together so many and such varied statistics as are contained in these tables is much labor, certainly enough to satisfy *one man* that a like experiment in book making would not be repeated without some misgivings.

In giving dates, the year only is stated, and not the day or the month. In this way there is greater uniformity,—for the month and the day, in many cases, could not be ascertained, and the year only is deemed sufficient.

During an unavoidable delay in getting this work ready for the Press, several ministers have come to the State, and commenced labor in the churches. Their names are included in this table of ministers, so that it extends somewhat into the year 1861. The same extension will be found in the statistics of churches and houses of worship.

Ministers.

TABLE:

Showing the Ministers who are *now in Wisconsin*, their native State, where educated, when ordained, when they came, and their present fields of labor.

NAMES.	NATIVE STATE.	WHERE EDUCATED.	WHEN ORD'ND	CAME TO WIS.	PRESENT FIELDS OF LABOR.
A. S Allen,	Mass.	N. E.	1839	1846	Black Earth & Middleton,
W. Armes,	Vt.	N. E.	1833	1840	Without ch'ge,
A. Barlow.	N. H.	N. E.	1843	1845	"
H. H. Benson,	Vt.	N. E.	1845	1844	Mineral Point,
S. S. Bicknell,	N. H.	N. E.	1838	1845	Koshkonong,
C. Boynton,	N. Y.	N. Y.	1851	1850	Watertown-
D. P. Brown,	Vt.	N. E.	1830	1849	Without ch'rge,
J. J. Bushnell,	Ct.	N. E.	....	1848	"
C. C. Cadwell,	N. Y.	Ohio.	1835	1838	Genoa, & Rich.
C. W. Camp,	Ct.	N. E.	1848	1849	Sheboygan,
F. H. Case,	Ct.	N. E.	1845	1842	Without chr'ge,
A. L. Chapin,	Ct.	N. Y.	1844	1843	Prest Beloit C,
N. C. Chapin,	Ct.	N. Y.	1851	1849	La Crosse,
L. Clapp,	Mass.	N. E.	1845	1845	Wauwatosa,
A. Clarke,	Mass.	N. E.	1849	1848	Hartford,
D. Clary,	Mass.	N. Y.	1829	1840	Ag't Home Mis,
O. P. Clinton,	Vt.	N. Y.	1835	1842	Vinland,
W. Cochran,	Vt.	N. Y.	1846	1845	Brodhead,
O. F. Curtis,	N. H.	N. E.	1830	1840	Em'rald Grove,
S. D. Darling,	Mass.	N. E.	1841	1850	Oakfield,
J. Emerson,	Ct.	N. E.	1860	1848	Prof. Beloit C.
H. Foote,	N. Y.	N. Y.	1839	1842	Waukesha,
L. Foote,	Vt.	N. Y.	1829	1847	Without ch'rge,
H. Freeman,	Vt.	N. E.	1843	1846	"
J. Gridley,	N. Y.	N. Y.	1835	1847	Somers,
L. Hall,	....	N. E.	1825	1838	Without ch'rge.

Ministers.

NAMES.	NATIVE STATE.	WHERE EDU-CATED.	WHEN ORD'ND	CAME TO WIS.	PRESENT FIELDS OF LABOR.
J. Jameson,	Scot.	....	1843	1849	Magnolia,
O. Johnson,	Mass.	N. E.	1843	1845	Without ch'rge,
M. P. Kinney.	N. Y.	N. Y.	1844	1841	Janesville,
D. Lamb,	Vt.	N. E.	1831	1847	Spring Vale,
A. D. Laughlin,	K. Y.	Wis.	1847	1846	Muscoda and Pleasant Hill,
T. Loomis,	N. Y.	Ill.	1845	1848	Without ch'rge,
H. Marsh,	N. Y.	N. Y.	1842	1842	"
C. W. Mathews,	Vt.	N. E.	1851	1848	Sun Prairie,
S. A. M'Ewan,	N. Y.	N. Y.	1837	1849	Without ch'rge,
N. Miller,	N. Y.	N. Y.	1841	1846	Princeton,
S. E. Miner,	N. Y.	N. Y.	1838	1841	Without ch'rge
J. J. Mitre,	N. Y.	N. Y.	1838	1841	Beaver Dam,
E. J. Montague,	Mass.	N. E.	1846	1846	Oconomowoc & Summit,
M. Montague,	Mass.	N. E.	1844	1844	Prin. Allen's G. Academy,
C. Morgan,	N. Y.	N. Y.	1843	1850	E. Troy,
E. Morris,	Eng.	Eng.	1840	1850	Munro,
J. A. Northrop,	N. Y.	N. Y.	1839	1844	Without ch'rge
H. M. Parmalee,	N. Y.	Ohio.	1842	1850	Oak Grove,
D. Pinkerton,	N. H.	N. E.	1845	1844	Without ch'rge
J. Reynard,	Eng.	Ill.	1851	1850	Shullsburg & Monticello,
L. Rogers,	N. H.	N. J.	1832	1841	Without ch'rge
E. D. Seward,	Ct.	N. E.	1843	1843	Lake Mills,
F. G. Sherrill.	N. Y.	N. Y.	1850	1850	Fulton,
R. R. Snow,	Ct.	N. E.	2845	1840	Rochester,
J. D. Stevens,	N. Y.	N. Y.	1837	1841	Caldwells Pra. Maquonego,
S. H. Thompson	Ohio.	Ohio.	1842	1843	Ples't Pra.
C. Warner,	N. Y.	N. Y.	1835	1843	Elk Grove,
J. W. Walcott,	N. H.	N. E.	- --	1850	Without ch'rge
M. Wells.	N. Y.	N. Y.	1845	1843	Necedah and Mauston.
H. Avery,	Ohio.	Ohio.	1860	1857	Stockbridge,

The foregoing ministers were in Wisconsin in 1850. See His. Chs., p. 90.

The following have come to Wisconsin since 1850, and are still here:

Ministers.

NAMES.	NATIVE STATE.	WHERE EDU-CATED.	WHEN ORD'ND	CAME TO WIS.	PRESENT FIELD OF LABOR.
W. F. Avery,	Mass.	N. E.	1855	1854	Without ch'rge
E. Bascom,	----	----	----	1857	Without ch'rge
D. M. Bardwell,	----	----	----	----	Ag. Bi. Soc.,
B. S. Baxter,	Vt.	Vt.	1841	1859	Burns & Leon,
F. W. Beecher,	Ill.	N. E.	1860	1860	Mil. Hanover st
W. Bigelow,	Vt.	N. E.	1854	1854	Black R. Falls.
A. Benton,	Ct.	Ohio.	1837	1855	Without ch'rge
D. H. Blake,	Vt.	N. Y.	1859	1860	Waupun,
J. J. Blaisdell,	N. H.	N. E.	1852	1859	Prof Beloit C.,
E. Brown,	Ct.	Ohio.	1853	1850	West Salem, N. La Crosse, Omalaska,
H. N. Brinsmade	Ct.	N. E.	1828	1853	1st C. Ch. Bel'it
S. Bristol,	Ct.	N. E.	1842	1852	Dartford and Metomen,
W. H. Burnard,	Eng.	Ill.	1854	1854	Shopiere & Cl.
D. A. Campbell,	Me.	West.	1852	1845	Richford & W.
P. Caufield,	----	----	----	1852	Menominee,
H. M. Chapin,	Vt.	N. E.	1855	1844	Markesan,
J. Collie,	Scot.	Wis.	1855	1854	Delavan,
G. W. Cotterell,	----	----	----	1854	Without ch'rge
J. N. Cundall,	Ct.	N. E.	1854	1854	Rosendale,
D. C. Curtiss,	Ct.	N. E.	1840	1855	Fort Atkinson,
W. Day,	----	----	----	----	Without ch'rge
D. S. Dickinson,	----	----	----	1861	Union Grove,
A. M. Dixon,	Ten.	Ill.	1842	1856	Blakes Prairie,
H. H. Dixon,	Vt.	Vt.	1852	1851	Without ch'rge
J. W. Donaldson	N. Y.	N. Y.	1858	1843	Kewaunee,
S. A. Dwinnell,	Mass.	Mass.	1853	1835	Reedsburg & V
F. B. Doe,	Vt.	N. E.	1854	1858	Appleton,
M. Doolittle,	----	----	----	1858	Darlington,
B. Durham.	Ohio.	Wis. & Ill.	----	1861	Evansville,

Ministers.

NAMES.	NATIVE STATE.	WHERE EDUCATED.	WHEN ORD'ND	CAME TO WIS.	PRESENT FIELD OF LABOR.
C. Ellis,	----	----	----	1859	Quincy and Rochacree.
R. Everdell.	Eng.	Eng.	1835	1850	Saxville, Poysippi, Auroraville,
E. N. Goddard,	----	N. E.		1861	Markesan,
N. D. Graves,	Mass.	Mass.	1846	1854	2d C. C. Beloit
J. Hall,	Eng.	Eng.	1848	1852	Brookfield,
H. Hanmer,	----	----	----	1855	Without ch'rge
R. Hassell,	Eng.	Eng.	1844	1846	Low'ille & L'ds
J. A. Hawley,	Ct.	Ct.	1841	1852	Ripon,
J. M. Hayes,	----	----	----	1856	Without ch'rge
C. D. Helmer,	N. Y.	Ct.	1859	1859	Plym. C. Mil.
T. B. Hulbert,	Vt.	N. Y.	1834	1860	Hammond,
S. J. Humphrey	N. H.	N. E.	1854	1861	Beloit 1st C. C.
C. J. Hutchins,	Pa.	Ct.	1855	1859	Racine,
H. Hutchens,	Eng.	Eng.	1857	1854	Sauk City,
F. M. Jams,	Ohio.	Ohio.	1860	1855	Tomah and Jacksonville,
J. S. Jenkens,	Eng.	L. C.	1860	1857	Merrimac & Caledonia,
G. C. Judson,	Ct.	Ohio.	1846	1859	Viroqua and Sterling,
J. Keep,	Mass.	N. E.	1835	1861	Bristol,
L. H. Kelsey,	N. Y.	N. E.	----	1860	Prof. Beloit C.
A. Kidder,	Vt.	N. Y.	1849	1856	Eau Claire,
B. King,	N. Y.	N Y.	1857	1860	Milton,
A. C. Lathrop,	Ct.	N .Y	1843	1853	Montello & Westfield,
W. D. S. Love,	N. Y.	N. Y.	1848	1857	Milwaukee,
N. McLeod,	Can.	L. C.	1849	1859	Prescott,
J. Manley,	----	----	----	1851	Without ch'rge
W. H, Marble,	N. H.	N. Y.	1850	1856	Oshkosh,
J. T Marsh,	Ct.	N. E.	1853	1857	Hartland,
L. E. Matson,	----	----	1861	1861	Racine,
J. T. Mathews,	Mass.	N. E.	1859	1859	Kenosha,
C. T. Melvin,	N. H.	N. E.	1859	1859	Columbus,
W. E. Merriman	Mass.	N. E.	1857	1861	Green Bay,

Ministers.

NAMES.	NATIVE STATE.	WHERE EDU-CATED.	WHEN ORD'ND	CAME TO WIS.	PRESENT FIELDS OF LABOR.
N. A. Millard,	N. Y.	N. Y.	....	1860	Raymond,
E. G. Miner,	Mass.	N. E.	1852	1851	Whitewater,
H. A. Miner,	Vt.	N. E.	1859	1857	Menasha,
C. M. Morehouse	N. Y.	N. Y.	1848	1864	Evansville,
W. J. Monteith,	N. Y.	N. Y.	1837	1856	Genesee,
D. T. Noyes,	Mass.	N. E.	1852	1851	Richland Co.,
A. A. Overton,	Ct.	Wis.	1857	1847	Avoca & Bos'll
L. Parker,	....	....	....	1861	Oconto Co.,
J. H. Payne,	N. Y.	N. Y.	1836	1858	Salem & Wilm't
E. S. Peck,	....	....	....	1853	W. C. O. S. Pr
S. D. Peet,	Ohio.	Wis. & Ill	1854	1856	Fox Lake,
J. W. Perkins,	N. H.	N. H.	1833	1857	Chester and Lawrence,
P. C. Pettibone,	N. Y.	N. Y.	1840	1856	Burlington,
D. Phillips,	Wales	N. E.	1861	1860	Sparta,
J. E. Pond,	Mass.	N. E.	1859	1858	Nenah,
W. Porter,	Mass.	N. E.	1847	1852	Prof. Beloit C.
L. L. Radcliff,	N. Y.	N. Y.	1842	1855	Desoto,
B. W. Reynolds,	....	....	....	1851	Without ch'rge
J. P. Richards,	Pa.	Ill.	....	1861	Caledonia & Oak Creek,
W. M. Richards,	Ct.	N. E.	1835	1859	Berlin,
E, W. Rice,	N. Y.	N. Y.	1860	1858	Ag't Sab. Sch.,
E. P. Salmon,	Mass.	N. J.	1831	1860	Allen's Grove,
A. Sedgwick,	Ct.	Mass.	1824	1858	Lafayette & Spring Prairie
R. Sewall,	Eng.	Eng.	1854	1853	Stoughton,
J. Silsby,	Pa.	P & O	1861	1861	Pra. du Sac,
J. C. Sherwin,	N. Y.	Ohio.	1840	1851	Ag't A. H.M.S.
J. B. L. Soule,	Me.	Me.	1858	1858	Elkhorn,
T. D. So'thworth	N. Y.	N. Y.	1832	1859	Williams,
W. R. Stevens,	Mass.	N. H.	1847	1855	River Falls & Malone,
W. Stoddart,	Sc'tl'd	Wis.	1857	1856	Fairplay,
L. Taylor,	Mass.	N. E.	1843	1861	Madison,
S. H. Thompson	....	Ohio.	....	1861	Pleasant Pra.
J. D. Todd,	N. Y.	Wis.	1860	1866	Sextonville,

Ministers.

NAMES.	NATIVE STATE.	WHERE EDU-CATED.	WHEN ORD'ND	CAME TO WIS.	PRESENT FIELD OF LABOR.
G. L. Tucker,	Vt.	Wis. & N. Y.	----	1859	Trempeleau,
E. B. Tuthill,	N. Y.	N. E.	1861	1861	Baraboo,
T.A Wadswo'th	Eng.	Ohio.	1854	1859	Sheboygan F'lls
J. K. Warner,	N. Y.	Ct.	1858	1859	Centre,
J. H. Waterman	N. Y.	N. Y.	1861	1860	Pewaukie,
.J Watts,	Eng.	N. Y.	----	1969	Johnstown,
B. H. Willi'ms'n	----	Mass.	1860	1858	Fond du Lac,
J. N. Woodruff,	N. Y.	Ohio.	1858	1860	Hudson.

Ministers.

TABLE:

Containing the names of Ministers who have labored in the State some part of the time the past ten years, and have left the State, when they came, where they labored, when when they went away, and where they went, so far as is known.

NAMES.	CAME TO WISC.	FIELD OF LABOR.	WENT AWAY	WHERE THEY WENT.
J. W. Allen,	1850	Marquette, S Falls,	1857	New Eng.
G. W. Bassett,	1850	Milwaukee, Free ch.	1851	Illinois.
E. G. Bradford,	1842	Waupun, Princeton,	1856	New Eng.
L. Bridgeman,	1842	Westfield,	1857	New Eng.
B. C. Church,	1745	Wyoming,	1857	Michig'n.
A. Eddy,	1849	Beloit,	1856	Illinois.
B. Foltz,	1849	Allens' G & Burling.	1858	"
J. E. Heaton,	1837	Waterloo,	1856	Nebraska.
W. Herritt,	1849	Manitowoc,	1853	Illinois.
T. M. Hopkins,	1845	Racine,	1859	New York
Z. M. Humphrey	1849	Racine, Mil., Plym.,	1859	Chicago.
J. H. Kassan,	1846	Markesan, Baraboo,	1855	Iowa.
A. Lilley.	1844	Hartland, Pewaukee,	1853	New York
C. Lord,	1846	Madison,	1854	New Eng.
H. Lyman,	1845	Sheboygan, Johnst'n	1854	New York
J. H. Martyn,	1850	Waukesha,	1853	"
C. W. Monroe,	1849	Howard, Appleton,	1856	Boston.
W. A. Niles,	1850	Beaver Dam, Water.	1859	N. Y.
M. Ordway.	1836	Without Charge.	1857	Rockfo'd.
W. L. Parsons,	1848	Milwaukee,	1853	New Eng.
J. M. Phillips,	1846	Hazel Green,	1852	Iowa.
J. Porter,	1840	Green Bay,	1858	Chicago.
L. Robbins,	1850	Omro,	1857	Iowa.
F. H. Rood,	1850	Sheboygan,	1851	Vermont.
W. J. Smith,	1848	Richland Co.,	1858	Iowa.
W. H. Spencer,	1850	Milwaukee,	1855	Philadel.

The foregoing Ministers were in the State in 1850. See His. of Chs, p. 90.

11

Ministers.

TABLE :

Containing a list of Ministers who have come to Wisconsin since 1850 and have left the State :

NAMES.	CAME TO WIS.	FIELDS OF LABOR.	WENT	WHERE GONE.
H. C. Atwater,	1859	Hartland,	1860	N. E.
W. S. Blanchard	1851	Sheboygan,	1852	....
G. M. Blauvelt,	1857	Racine,	1859	New Jersey,
H. W. Brown,	1859	Ripon,	1860	East,
B. Burnap,	1853	Hazel Green,	1854	N. Y.
J. Caldwell,	1859	Madison,	1860	....
E.B.Chamberlin	1859	Green Bay,	1860	N. Y.
H. W. Cobb,	1856	Prescott,	1857	Ill.
W. F. Clarke,	1857	Waukesha,	1859	Canada,
T. Cook,	1854	Menasha,	1856	N. E.
O. W. Cooley,	1853	Fox Lake, N. Port and K. City,	1858	Ill.
J. Cushman,	1851	Elkhorn & Pewaukee	1854	N. E.
S. Day,	1857	Milwaukee,	1859	Ill.
W. P. Davis,	1857	Rochester & Wat'rfrd	1858	N. Y.
— Dickinson,	1858	Kenosha,	1859	Ill.
C. B. Donalson,	1858	Lowell & Waukesha,	1860	Ill.
N. H. Eggleston	1857	Madison,	1860	Mass.
J. S. Emery,	1854	Sheb. Falls, Union Grove & Palmyra,	1858	Ill.
S. Emerson,	1853	Genesee,	1854	South,
F. W. Fisk,	1853	Beloit Coll., Prof.	1858	Chicago Sem.
N. C. Goodhue,	1851	Jefferson & Koskon'g	1857	East,
F. Harman,	1854	Hartl'nd &Pewaukee	1855	Iowa,
W. S. Huggins,	1852	Beloit & Whitewater,	1854	Mich.
J. G. Hibbard,	1856	Salem & Wilmot,	1858	Ill.
S. Hawley,	1853	Fond du Lac,	1858	N. Y.
L. H. Johnson,	1856	Elkhorn,	1859	Rockford, Ill.
Chas. Jones,	1860	Platteville,	1861	N. E.
J. Laughran,	1856	Hazel Green,	1858	...;

Ministers.

NAMES.	CAME TO WIS.	FIELDS OF LABOR.	WENT	WHERE GONE.
F. Lawson,	1853	Fulton, Evansville & P. Pra.	1860	Ill.
E. M Lewis,	1858	Potosi & Rockville,	1860	Mich.
T. Lyman,	1856	N. Pepin,	1858	....
W. L. Mather,	1855	Fond du Lac, Plymouth & Geneva,	1861	Chaplain in Army,
C. H. Marshall,	1858	Hudson,	1859	....
H. B. Pierpont,	1857	Two Rivers,	1860	Mich.
B. B. Parsons,	1857	Ripon,	1859	Ill.
D. W. Pickard,	1858	Platteville,	1859	Maine,
J. A. Roberts,	1859	Sparta,	1859	....
W, Scofield,	1858	Janesville,	1859	Ill.
G. Spaulding,	1854	Genesee, Baraboo & Hammond,	1860	Min.
M. C. Stanley,	1856	Two Rivers and Manitowoc,	1859	Mich.
Ira Tracy,	1851	Blake's Pra. & vic.,	1856	Min.
W. W. Warner,	1857	Dodgeville,	1858	N. Y.
A. Warren,	1853	Milton,	1857	Ill.
J. Wilcox,	1851	Pakwaukee & vicin.	1858	Ohio.

Ministers

Who have died in Wisconsin.

NAMES.	CAME TO WIS.	FIELD OF LABOR.	DIED.	AGE.
W. Adams,	1837	Beloit & Mineral Point,	1842	53
N. Kingsbury,	1840	S. Prairieville,	1843	46
D. A. Sherman,	1840	East Troy & Pike Grove,	1843	62
S. Hubbard,	1840	Without charge,	1846	65
Edward Allen,	1846	Fulton,	1846	51
F. H. Pitkin,	1845	Delavan,	1847	27
Eber Child,	1846	Fulton,	1847	48
A. D. Harris,	1849	Without charge,	1850	29
Wm. Marchant,	1844	" "	1850	52
A. Gaston,	....	Delavan and vicinity,	1849	40
C. L. Adams,	1850	Neenah,	1852	33
C. A. Boardman,	1854	Monroe,	1860	72
S. Chaffee,	1840	Richland county,	1856	..
T. G. Cole,	1856	Centre,	1857	34
C. Eddy,	1859	Without charge,	1861	66
E. S. Hunter,	1851	" "	1858	62
J. Lewis,	1843	Platteville,	1860	43
J. O. Knapp,	1859	2d Cong. Ch., Beloit,	1860	..
C. C. Mason,	1852	Centre, joined Methodist,	1858	..
A. Montgomery,	1856	Agent A. B. C. F. M.	1859	..
J. Morton,	1854	Sheboygan county,	1859	..
S. Peet,	1837	Ag't Chicago Theo. Sem.	1855	58
O. S. Powell,	1850	Fort Atkinson,	1855	..
C.E. Rosenkrans	1842	Columbus,	1861	..
J. D. Strong,	1856	Lowville,	1859	..
W. H. Spencer,	1851	Died at Chicago,	1861	..
M. Steel,	1851	Died at the East,	....	30
D. W. Pickard,	1853	Died in Maine,	1859	..
D. Lamb,	1847	Springvale,—Aug.	1861	..
N. Miller,	1846	Princeton, "	1861	..

HISTORY OF CHURCHES.

Explanation.

The plan adopted in giving a history of the churches is similar to that in the history of ministers.

This part of the work in hand may appear to some to be unnecessary after having the main facts given so fully and so recently in the published minutes of the General Convention. In reply to such a suggestion, if made, it may be proper to state,

1st. That the minutes are but yearly histories. This is a summary for the past ten years.

2d. The minutes of the Convention have been published but eight years since 1850, and the statistics of many of the churches are frequently wanting in the minutes when published.

3d. There are several churches whose date of organization is more or less recent, and which sympathize and cooperate with the American Home Missionary Society, and yet are not at present connected with the Convention; therefore the minutes contain no reports from them, and they should be included in this history.

The names of those churches which have united with presbyteries since the former history was published are omitted here; also the names of Welch churches, connected with the Convention. Both will be found in their respective connections.

A full history of the churches might require that the names of all their ministers since 1850 should be given, with the length of time which each one has labored with them. But to do this is not practicable, without materially changing the form of this work; therefore are given the names only of the ministers who are now supplying them.

In some cases churches have become extinct, and, after a few years, organizations have been effected at or near the same places, and under the same name, form of government, and in the same ecclesiastical connection.

Such cases remain without any notice of this feature in their history. The church is deemed essentially the same.

CHURCHES.

TABLE:

Containing the names of churches now in the State, their form of government, date of organization, increase of members the past ten years, and the names of ministers now laboring with them. The first in order are the names of churches that were in the State in 1850; then those that have been organized since that time.

NAMES.	GOV.	WHEN ORG.	MEMBERS 1850	MEMBERS 1860	MINISTERS.
Allen's Grove,	C	1845	70	147	E. P. Salmon,
Alto,	C	1849	17	29	
Appleton,	P	1850	8	116	F. B. Doe,
Aztalan,	C	1840	25	..	Extinct,
Baraboo,	C	1847	34	39	Vacant,
Beaver Dam,	P	1843	93	161	J. J. Mitre,
Beetown,	C	1847	20	11	N. Wayne,
Beloit 1st,	C	1838	207	303	S. J. Humphrey,
Big Platte,	P	1842	13	..	Extinct,
Blakes' Prairie,	P	1847	28	73	A. M. Dixon,
Bower Branch,	C	1849	14	17	Vacant,
Bloomfield, now Genoa,	C	1846	14	51	C. C. Cadwell,
Bristol,	C	1851	12	36	J. Keep,
Brookfield,	C	1849	15	21	J. Hall,
Burlington, now Union C.	P	1848	18	75	P. C. Pettibone,
Byron,	C	1849	7	..	Extinct,
Caledonia,	C	1844	13	14	J. P. Richards,
Centre,	C	1844	24	56	J. K. Warner,
Cereso, now Ripon,	C	1851	11	153	J. A. Hawley,
Clyman,	C	1844	9	..	Extinct,
Dartford,	C	1849	7	57	S. Bristol,
Delafield,	P	1849	18	6	Vacant,

Churches.

NAMES.	GOV.	WHEN ORG.	MEMBERS 1850	MEMBERS 1860	MINISTERS.
Delavan,	C	1841	88	158	J. Collie,
Dodgeville,	C	1847	43	41	Vacant,
Dunkirk,	C	1846	12	..	Extinct.
East Troy,	P	1839	25	78	C. Morgan,
Elk Grove,	C	1846	32	72	C. Warner,
Elkhorn,	C	1843	45	45	J. B. L. Soule,
Emerald Grove,	C	1846	29	116	O. F. Curtis,
Evansville 1st,	C	1846	26	..	Excluded,
Exeter,	C	1849	9	..	Extinct,
Fairfield, now Oak Grove,	C	1849	23	53	H. M. Parmalee,
Fairplay,	P	1842	19	30	W. Stoddart,
Fond du Lac,	C	1842	57	..	R. H. Williamson,
Fountain Pra.,	C	1847	17	..	Extinct,
Franklin,	P	1845	8	..	Extinct,
Fort Atkinson,	C	1841	48	68	D. C. Curtiss,
Genesee,	C	1842	61	41	W. J. Monteith,
Geneva,	P	1839	76	175	W. L. Mather,
Granville,	C	1843	15	..	Extinct,
Green Bay,	P	1836	84	94	W. C. Merriman,
Hartford,	C	1847	12	68	A. Clarke,
Hazel Green,	P	1845	50	15	H. Maibin,
Janesville,	C	1845	100	258	M. P. Kinney,
Johnstown,	C	1845	31	53	J. Watts,
Kenosha,	C	1838	170	191	J. T. Matthews,
Koskonong,	C	1846	17	42	S. S. Bicknell,
Lake Mills,	C	1847	36	80	E. D. Seward,
La Martine,	C	1850	10	..	Extinct,
Lancaster,	C	1843	46	47	S. W. Eaton,
Lisbon 1st,	C	1842	35	..	Extinct,
Lisbon 2d,	C	1848	14	..	Extinct,
Lowell,	C	1845	12	25	H. M. Parmalee,
Madison,	C	1840	40	57	L. Taylor,
Marquette co. now Markesan	P	1847	7	20	E. N. Goddard,
Milton,	C	1838	37	43	B. King,
Milwaukee, Ply.	C	1841	175	335	C. D. Helmer,

Churches.

NAMES.	GOV.	WHEN ORG.	MEMBERS 1850	MEMBERS 1860	MINISTERS.
Mil. Free ch., now Spring st.	C	1847	52	203	W. D. L. Love,
Mineral Point,	P	1839	75	66	H. H. Benson,
Mt. Zion,	C	1842	28	..	Extinct,
Monroe, Reorg. & Con.	P	1850	18	26	E. Morris,
Neenah, now Presbyt.,	C	1846	29	96	J. E. Pond,
Newark,	C	1845	29	..	Extinct,
New Diggings,	C	1844	21	..	Extinct,
N. Rochester,	C	1840	40	25	J. D. Stevens,
Oak Creek, ex.,	C	1846	10	..	J. P. Richards,
Oakfield,	C	1848	15	18	S. D. Darling,
Oconomowoc,	C	1845	25	62	E. J. Montague,
Ohio Settlement	C	1847	12	..	Extinct,
Oshkosh,	C	1849	41	260	W. H. Marble,
Palmyra,	P	1847	29	45	H. T. Lathrop,
Paris, now Union Grove,	C	1844	42	35	J. S. Dickinson,
Pewaukee,	C	1840	33	33	J. H. Waterman,
Pike Grove, now Somers,	P	1839	34	42	J. Gridley,
Platteville,	C	1839	128	149	Vacant,
Pleasant Pra.,	C	1844	39	20	S. H. Thompson,
Potosi,	P	1840	32	19	Vacant,
Pra. du Chien,	P	1842	..	25	Vacant,
Pra. du Sac,	C	1841	19	27	J. Silsby,
Racine,	P	1839	191	218	C. J. Hutchins,
Racine,	C	1850	40	83	L. E. Matson,
Raymond,	P	1840	88	49	N. A. Millard,
Richland, or Buena Vista,	P	1850	11	30	J. D. Todd,
Richmond, now Orion,	P	1850	14	14	A. D. Laughlin,
Ridgeway,	P	1845	39	..	Extinct,
Rochester,	C	1840	39	23	J. D. Stevens,
Rosendale,	C	1848	30	100	I. N. Cundall,

Churches.

NAMES.	GOV.	WHEN ORG.	MEMBERS 1850	MEMBERS 1860	MINISTERS.
Salem,	C	1840	38	31	J. H. Payne,
Sheboygan,	C	1845	43	61	C. W. Camp,
Sheboygan,	P	1850	20	..	Extinct,
Sheb. Falls,	C	1847	72	58	T. H. Wadsworth,
Shopiere,	C	1844	81	161	W. H. Burnard,
Stockbridge, Indian,	P	1830	..	..	Removed,
Shulsburg,	C	1848	18	42	J. Raynard,
Spring Prairie,	C	1841	23	14	A. Sedgwick,
Springvale,	C	1848	45	45	D. Lamb,
Sugar Creek,	C	1841	30	..	Extinct,
Summit,	P	1841	37	62	E. J. Montague,
Sun Prairie,	C	1846	11	25	C. W. Matthews,
Troy,	C	1839	71	21	Vacant,
Vinland,	C	1850	9	17	O. P. Clinton,
Warren, now Hartland,	C	1841	21	72	J. T. Marsh,
Waterloo,	C	1845	20	13	Vacant,
Watertown,	C	1845	21	130	C. Boynton,
Waukesha,	C	1838	98	110	H. Foote,
Waupun,	C	1845	31	82	D. H. Blake,
Wauwatosa,	C	1842	31	88	L. Clapp,
Whitewater,	C	1840	97	166	E. G. Miner,
Willow Springs,	C	1847	19	..	Extinct,
Wyoming,	P	1846	41	57	Vacant,
Yellow Stone,	C	1848	20	..	Extinct.

Churches.

The following churches have been organized since 1850:

NAMES.	GOV.	WHEN ORG.	MEMBERS THEN	MEMBERS NOW	MINISTERS.
Albany,	C	1853	10	25	J. Jameson,
Argyle,	C	1854	12	..	Extinct,
Auroraville,	C	1857	12	15	R. Everdell,
Avoca,	C	1858	8	11	A. A. Overton,
Barre,	C	1858	15	12	E. Brown,
Beloit 2d,	C	1859	46	64	N. D. Graves,
Black Earth,	C	1856	11	13	A. S. Allen,
Black R. Falls,	C	1855	9	10	W. Bigelow,
Boscobell,	C	1857	6	12	A. A. Overton,
Brodhead,	C	1859	27	61	W. Cochran,
Burns,	C	1858	8	42	B. S. Baxter,
Charlestown,	C	1861	10	13	H. Avery,
Chester,	C	1858	5	17	J. W. Perkins,
Clinton,	C	1858	35	61	W. H. Burnard,
Cooksville, now Stought'n	P	1851	15	34	R. Sewell,
Darlington,	C	1856	11	72	M. Doolittle,
Dayton,	P	1858	12	14	J. D. Todd,
De Soto,	C	1856	10	7	L. L. Radcliff,
Dover,	C	1854	12	23	Vacant,
East Ithaca,	C	1859	8	17	J. D. Todd,
Eau Claire,	C	1856	6	22	A. Kidder,
Empire,	C	1855	9	..	Extinct,
Evansville 2d,	C	....	5	50	B. Durham,
Fond du Lac,	C	1856	35	149	R. H. Williamson,
Fox Lake,	C	1853	8	65	S. D. Peet,
Fulton,	C	1851	9	61	F. G. Shirrell,
Grand Rapids,	C	1860	6	6	Vacant,
Green Lake,	C	1853	11	14	H. M. Chapin,
Hammond,	C	1858	15	25	T. B. Hurlbut,
Hortonville,	C	1852	11	17	O. P. Clinton,
Howard,	C	1855	6	12	Vacant,
Hudson,	C	1857	17	49	L. N. Woodruff,
Hustisford,	C	1857	8	8	Vacant,
Ironton,	C	1860	9	9	S. A. Dwinnell,
Jefferson,	C	1851	9	..	Extinct,

Churches.

NAMES.	GOV.	WHEN ORG.	MEMBERS THEN	MEMBERS NOW	MINISTERS.
Jacksonville,	C	1860	10	15	F. M. Iams,
Kilbourn city,	C	1858	14	14	Vacant,
La Crosse,	C	1852	12	77	N. C. Chapin,
Lafayette,	C	1855	20	44	A. Sedgwick,
Leon,	C	1860	27	40	B. S. Baxter,
Madison, Union,	C	1859	..	..	Vacant,
Magnolia,	C	1851	8	16	J. Jameson,
Malone,	C	1860	9	9	W. R. Stevens,
Maple Grove,	C	1853	14	43	J. C. Holmes,
Maquonego,	C	1857	9	15	J. D. Stevens,
Marquette,	C	1852	6	..	Extinct,
Mauston,	C	1858	6	7	M. Wells,
Mazo Manie,	C	1857	7	7	Vacant,
Menekaune,	P	1857	5	9	L. Parker,
Metomen,	C	1857	14	31	S. Bristol,
Merrimac,	C	1858	10	10	J. S. Jenkins,
Menasha,	C	1851	19	82	H. A. Miner,
Middleton,	C	1851	12	27	A. S. Allen,
Milwaukee, Hanover st.,	C	1861	29	51	F. W. Beecher,
Monticello,	P	1851	16	24	J. Reynard,
Muscoda,	C	1857	6	9	A. D. Laughlin,
New Lisbon,	C	1857	4	26	Vacant,
New London,	C	1857	13	32	Vacant,
Necedah,	C	1858	9	17	M. Wells,
Newport,	C	1855	10	15	Vacant,
North Pepin,	C	1856	14	20	Vacant,
North La Crosse	C	1859	9	15	E. Brown,
Oconto,	P	1858	7	9	L. Parker,
Onalaska,	C	1859	10	10	E. Brown,
Oxford,	C	1861	13	13	A. C. Lathrop,
Pakwaukee,	C	1852	8	..	Extinct,
Pleasant Hill,	P	1853	18	51	A. D. Laughlin,
Plover,	C	1859	14	23	Vacant,
Plymouth,	C	1854	14	42	T. A. Wadsworth,
Prescott,	C	1852	9	87	N. M. Lead,
Princeton,	C	1852	14	16	N. Miller,

Churches.

NAMES.	GOV.	WHEN ORG.	MEMBERS THEN	MEMBERS NOW	MINISTERS.
Quincy,	C	1858	7	10	Vacant,
Richford,	C	1858	17	24	D. A. Campbell,
Richland City,	C	1855	19	17	J. D. Todd,
Ridgeway,	C	1856	12	--	Extinct,
Reedsburg,	C	1851	16	44	S. A. Dwinnell,
River Falls,	C	1855	16	80	W. R. Stevens,
Roch a Cree,	C	1858	8	8	Vacant,
Rockville,	C	1853	5	12	Vacant,
Rugglesville,	C	1856	12	--	Extinct,
Saxville,	C	1858	10	17	R. Everdell,
Sparta,	C	1855	22	58	D. Phillips,
Spring Green,	C	1859	11	12	D. T. Noyes,
Sterling,	C	1859	10	10	G. C. Judson,
Stockbridge,	C	1860	15	20	H. Avery,
Stone Bank,	P	1852	14	26	J. Conly,
Stoughton,	P	1851	15	34	R. Sewell,
Teychedah,	C	1854	10	2	Extinct,
Tomah,	C	1859	11	23	F. M. Iams,
Trempeleau,	C	1857	13	25	G. L. Tucker,
Two Rivers,	C	1852	10	38	Vacant,
Viroqua,	C	1855	7	16	G. C. Judson,
Waterford,	C	1858	21	23	J. D. Stevens,
Wautoma,	C	1853	5	22	D. A. Campbell,
Waukau,	C	1858	16	7	T. A. Amerman,
Westfield,	C	1852	8	30	A. C. Lathrop,
West Salem,	C	1860	10	10	E. Brown,
Williams,	C	1859	12	21	T. D. Southworth,
Wilmot,	C	1851	10	18	J. H. Payne,
Windsor,	C	1851	7	35	C. W. Matthews,
Wyalusing,	C	1854	--	--	Extinct,
Wyocena,	C	1853	20	70	S. H. Barteau,
Wyota,	P	1854	16	4	Extinct.

Churches.

Of the foregoing churches, the following are extinct, viz:

Aztalan,	Lisbon 1st,	Yellow Stone,
Big Platte,	Lisbon 2d,	Argyle,
Byron,	Mount Zion,	Empire,
Clyman,	Newark,	Marquette,
Dunkirk,	New Diggings,	Pakwaukee,
Exeter,	Oak Creek,	Teychedah,
Evansville,	Ohio Settlement,	Wyalusing,
Fountain Prairie,	Ridgeway P.,	Wyota,
Franklin,	Ridgeway C.,	Stockbridge,
Grandville,	Rugglesville,	Jefferson,
Lamartine,	Sheboygan P.,	Sugar Creek.

SUMMARY.

Whole number of churches organized before 1850,.......		111
" " " since 1850,......		101
Total,..................................		212
Extinct, of those organized in 1850,.................	23	
" " since 1850,................	10	33
		179
Welch churches,..................................		20
Total now,..............................		199

CAUSES OF THE EXTINCTION.

Among the causes, and perhaps the most prominent, may be the following:

1. The loss by death or by emigration of the leading members:

2. Inability to obtain ministers.

3. Changes of central points, and the organization of churches near where there was more rapid growth and increase of population and business, and consequently greater privileges.

4. Perhaps premature organization.

Failures like these, especially in new regions which are being rapidly settled, and are subject to many fluctuations and changes, may occur in spite of the wisest forecast and the greatest care.

Many, and perhaps all, of these extinct churches had been fostered, as far as was practicable, by ministers residing nearest to them, and by home missionary aid.

Some of them had attained to considerable strength, as will be seen from the fact that the aggregate membership by the last reports was over 500, and that eight of them had houses of worship.

By comparing the number of extinct churches with the whole number organized, it will be seen that the proportion has greatly diminished the past ten years.

In a very few instances, where churches of two or more denominations had existed, and become nearly or quite extinct, the few remaining members have united in one organization, and, by way of accommodation, have taken the name of Union Congregational Church. But in no case, so far as is known, has this union included any except such as are recognized as orthodox in sentiment, and such as we were accustomed to fellowship as Christians.

Welch Ministers and Churches.

MINISTERS.	CAME TO WIS.	CHURCHES.	WHEN ORG.	MEM-BERS THEN	MEM-BERS NOW
J. Davies,	1854	Bangor,	1855	12	39
"		Fish Creek,	1859	20	26
J. Davis,		Rosendale,	1851	9	35
G. Griffiths,	1857	Milwaukee,	1857	8	32
"		Delafield,	1844	12	57
D. Jones,	1844	Without charge,	----	--	--
G. Jones,		Cambria,	1859	25	50
"		Welch Pra.,	1848	19	80
J. P. Jones,	1852	Spring Green,	----	--	80
W. W. Jones,	1855	Spring Water,	1853	11	28
D. Lewis,	1849	Ridgeway and	1853	21	59
"		Blue Mounds,	1847	9	33
R. Morris,	1846	Without charge,	----	--	--
E. Owens,		Bethel and	1857	21	25
"		Dodgeville,	1845	19	48
G. Samuel,		Emmet,	1846	16	30
"		Ixonia,	1856	25	22
R. Williams,		Rehoboth,	1850	20	21
— Hopkins,		Racine,	1848	21	100
"		Pike Grove,	1852	42	80
"		Bark River,	1859	50	55
H. Parry,	1861	Oshkosh,	1850	16	20

These Welch churches and ministers are Congregational in sentiment, differing in nothing essential from American Congregationalists. The most of them belong to the Convention. Nine of the fourteen ministers, and twelve of the twenty churches are in this connection. They also belong to an association of their own. This privilege is extended to them for their benefit. They are becoming Americanized very fast, and at no distant day they will probably discontinue their separate organization.

They are in full sympathy with the American Home Missionary Society, and all these churches are or have been aided by the Society in the support of their ministers. The total number of members in these twenty churches is nine hundred and twenty.

Most of the ministers received their education in Wales, and have come to this country within a few years past.

All these churches have houses of worship. In building them they have been very economical. Six of them are built of logs, costing from eighty to one hundred dollars each. The other fourteen have cost on an average about four hundred dollars. The most expensive one is at Milwaukee, and cost less than fourteen hundred dollars.

A few of the churches were aided in building these houses from the Congregational Building Fund.

PART III.

HOME MISSIONS.

The author of the former history of churches in Wisconsin, near the close of the book, page 189, gives a brief statement of what had been accomplished in the State up to that time, 1850, and of the influence of Home Missions in securing those results. He says :

"The history of the rise and progress of religious institutions in this State is without a parallel in respect to their early establishment and their rapid advancement.

"Fifteen years ago this country was occupied by the wild red man and the wild prey which he followed in the chase.

"In 1836, one minister entered this field and commenced his labors, and one church was organized during that year.

"In 1839, when the writer passed over the Territory and explored its situations and wants, he found three ministers and five or six churches. From that time there has been a constant accession of ministers and a rapid increase of churches, from year to year. There are now on this ground one hundred ministers and one hundred and twenty-five churches. An ecclesiastical organization has been established, consisting of a General Convention and four District Conventions, which happily unite these churches and ministers in one body; and over forty houses of public worship have been erected.

"But these statistics and general statements by no means show what has been accomplished. An amount of moral influence has been exerted by these ministers and churches on the forming character of this young and growing State, which no arithmetic can compute and no mere figures can express. The Gospel has been preached, not only to congregations connected with these churches, but to multitudes in other places, and in the scattered settlements of the country. Sabbath schools have been extensively established, and multitudes of children and youth have thus been brought under religious instruction. The temperance cause has been aided and borne forward in its achievements. The Bible has been widely circulated. Tracts and religious books have been scattered over the state. The observance of the Sabbath has been promoted; the cause of education has been advanced; common schools have been encouraged, select schools and academies have been established and sustained, and a college has been founded and put in successful operation that is adequate to the wants of the country in this respect; and, what is more than all, revlvals of religion have been enjoyed among the churches, from year to year, which have resulted in the hopeful conversion of nearly three thousand souls.

"These happy results are to be traced in a great measure to the influence and efforts of the American Home Missionary Society.

"The early occupancy of the field by that society, its efficient aid and continued fostering care have placed the cause of religion in its present advantageous position in the State.

"Nearly all the churches in the State were either organized by the missionaries of that society, or have been aided in the support of its ministers by its funds.

"Most of the ministers who have labored in this field have received their support, in part, from this source. The whole number who have been aided by this society from the beginning is one hundred and twenty, of whom thirty have removed to fields of labor out of the State, eight have ceased to receive aid, and five have gone to their reward on high.

"Ten churches once aided by this society now support their own ministers.

"Those ministers who are now sustained by their own people are occupying ground prepared to their hands by the A. H. M. Society, and building on foundations laid by them.

"The whole amount of funds which this society has expended in Wisconsin is about sixty-five thousand dollars. The whole number of ministers aided is one hundred and twenty. The years of labor performed are four hundred and twenty."

Growth of the Field.

The successor of Rev. Mr. Peet in the Agency of Home Missions entered upon his labors the 1st of August, 1850. At that time there were very few settlers north of Fox river, and north and west of Wisconsin river. The Indians' title to the land was but recently extinguished. The Indians themselves still occupied large portions of it. But little of it was in market.

The only churches organized beyond Fox river were Oshkosh and Neenah. North and west of Wisconsin river were the churches of Baraboo, Prairie du Sac, Buena Vista and Richmond. The village of La Crosse was not commenced.

The population in Wisconsin in 1850 was three hundred and five thousand five hundred and sixty-six. The number of organized counties was twenty-nine.

The tide of immigration, which had been checked for a time, greatly increased. New settlements were rapidly made. Material for new organizations accumulated. Internal improvements were commenced in the older settlements, and greater facilities were being furnished for reaching the newer parts of the State. As a consequence, new demands were created for Home Missionary labor.

More than two years had passed since Mr. Peet closed his labors as Agent of Home Missions, and during that time there was no agent in the State.

Labor of Agents.

Mr. Peet had been accustomed to give a large share of his labors to the organization of churches. But there were peculiar circumstances growing out of denominational relations, which made it expedient that, for the present, the responsibility of organizing churches should rest mainly on neighboring ministers and missionaries.

Those who have been accustomed to regard the work of agents at the East as consisting mainly in soliciting contributions, and at the West that of organizing churches and preaching to those that are destitute of ministers, have often inquired what constitutes the necessity of employing an agent where so little can be expected from the churches in the form of contributions, and where it is deemed expedient that he leave to others the main work of organizing churches. It may not be out of place, therefore, to give here a brief reply to such an inquiry. The following have been the principal features of the work in Wisconsin the past ten years, viz:

To explore the field, and learn its condition and wants;

To prepare the way for, and, when necessary, to assist in the organization of churches; or, if the way was found prepared, and the case seemed to require it, to organize churches himself;

To advise with and assist missionaries who were just entering new fields, in arranging their labors;

To visit destitute churches, preach to them and obtain supplies for them;

To act on application from churches for aid in support of their ministers; in doing which, it is expected that he will give the society what information he can relative to the need of aid, the amount that it would be wise to appropriate, and the general aspects of the field where funds are to be expended;

To visit missionaries, for the purpose of encouraging and assisting them in their labors and difficulties;

To render service, when desired, to ministers who wish to change their fields of labor, and to churches who wish to obtain ministers;

To present the claims of Home Missions to the churches, and to aid and encourage them in the development of their resources;

To correspond with the society relative to all that pertains to the work and the interests of Home Missions on the field;

To receive and distribute reports, books, tracts, boxes of clothing, &c., that are sent him; besides doing an indefinite amount of miscellaneous work.

The different kinds of work devolving on an agent vary in their proportions with the varying state of things in his field of labor. For example, there is now much less to be done in the way of exploring new regions and effecting new organizations; and more in that of developing the resources of the churches.

One agent occupied the whole state from 1850 to 1857, when the field became so wide and the work so great that the State was divided, and another agent was appointed for that portion of it which lies north and west of Wisconsin river.

The present extent of the whole field, compared with what it was in 1850, may be understood by the fact that there are now fifty-six organized counties, instead of twenty-nine, and a population of seven hundred and seventy-five thousand and six hundred, in place of three hundred and five thousand, an increase in ten years of full one hundred per cent., and the work of agents, though varying in its proportions, has increased accordingly.

Missionaries.

The work of supplying the State with missionaries, which was so early commenced and so successfully prosecuted from the beginning until 1850, as already quoted from the former history, has been continued to the present time.

New fields open have been occupied. New wants have been met. The missionaries have had ample scope for their energies and zeal, and great encouragements in their labors.

The number of missionaries has increased from year to year. Many have become pastors of churches. Many changes have taken place. Circumstances which appeared to be beyond human control have caused considerable fluctuation. Settlements, when made, have sometimes been of short continuance. Missionaries have come and labored a few years and left. Others have taken their places.

Not a few have moved on with the tide of emigration Westward. Others, overtaxing themselves with labor and care have been laid aside. Some have "fallen asleep," and "rest from their labors."

The number of commissions given by the A. H. M. Society to missionaries in the State, from 1851 to 1861, is nine hundred and twenty-eight.

The number of missionaries is as follows:

In 1851	84	In 1856	84
In 1852	83	In 1857	93
In 1853	87	In 1858	102
In 1854	100	In 1859	108
In 1855	87	In 1860	100

These statistics are taken from the annual reports of the Society, the report of each year being regarded as covering the preceding year which closes on the 1st of March, previous to the date of the report.

To give a statement of the results of the labors of these missionaries the past ten years, would only be to repeat what is stated in the former history, adding the increased proportions according as the number of missionaries has increased.

The season of great financial depression which has been experienced over all the land, and especially in the States of the North-West, has borne hard upon the missionaries. By reason of it many have learned, if they had not before, "how to be abased." But they have been content to share with the churches and with the community in general, the inconveniences and privations produced by it, and to labor on in the confident expectation that God will provide.

Missionary Churches.

In the former history it is stated that of the one hundred and twenty-six churches in the State in 1850, only ten supported their ministers without aid.

Since then the number of churches organized is one hundred and forty-one. Of these, one hundred and twelve will be found in the list of churches connected with the Convention including Welch churches, and twenty-nine in the list of churches connected with the Synod of Wisconsin.

The present number of self-supporting churches is forty. The others are dependent on Home Missionary aid. Of these, a few have received aid from the American Missionary Association, and three or four, so far as is known, from the Home Missionary Committee of the General Assembly.

Several German and Norwegian churches have been organized and aided in the course of the ten years, but at present none of them, except two Norwegian, are receiving aid. One church of Hollanders will be found connected with the Convention, and one with the Synod, that receive aid.

Appropriations and Contributions.

The statistics presented in the follow table are simple facts of history, which brethren consulted on the subject have thought might appropriately be placed in this connection. They may be instructive tor good in time to come, and furnish, in the review, cause for both gratitude and humility.

If, to any, the amounts contributed by the churches seem small in proportion to what has been received. and the progress towards self-support slow, it should be remembered that the early emigrants to a new country are generally poor, and besides large outlay to secure homes, and provide for domestic wants, they are taxed at once with the whole burden of necessary public improvements, Also, that the claims of the various objects of benevolence brought before them must not be set aside.

The aggregate of contributions to the objects of benevolence the past ten years, as stated in the very imperfect reports to the Convention, is $58,062.80.

This table, prepared originally by request of the H. M. Society and commenced with 1850, has been brought down to March, the close of the last Home Missionary year, making in all eleven years. The churches being then arranged according to their local and special relations, they are placed in the same order here.

Milwaukee Convention.

CHURCHES.	TOTAL AID.	TOTAL CONTRIB.
Milwaukee, Plymouth	$........	$719 82
Milwaukee, Spring st.	....	......
Wauwatosa	483 33	214 37
Brookfield	1,000 00	102 02
Pewaukee	414 58	15 91
Genesee	1,510 42	106 62
Delafield	887 50	37 30
Summit	....	27 00
Oconomowoc	812 30	72 67
Hartland	448 00	41 50
Newburg	279 50	23 04
Lisbon, extinct	500 00	27 96
Hartford	1,414 50	131 50
Kenosha	....	250 49
Salem	400 02	43 50
Wilmot	200 00	4 00
Pleasant Prairie	117 76	6 05
Somers	287 50	48 00
Paris	1,042 50	41 15
Racine, Presbyterian	....	668 23
Racine, Congregational	....	42 00
Burlington	350 00	15 62
Rochester	725 00	27 67
North Rochester	537 50	22 18
Raymond	450 00	46 55
Caledonia	677 42	27 64
Waterford	400 00	6 35
Oak Creek, extinct	675 42	4 00
Williams Ch.	175 00	10 00
Maquonego	75 00	7 50
Waukesha	....	5 00
Milwaukee, Hanover st.	....	....

Beloit Convention.

CHURCHES.	TOTAL AID.	TOTAL CONTRIB.
Beloit, 1st Congregational	$-------	$1,116 45
Janesville	158 33	228 61
Johnstown	951 67	82 33
Mount Zion, extinct	241 60	2 00
Shopiere	499 16	128 95
Milton	616 63	56 97
Fulton	740 00	36 00
Evansville	1,040 00	72 25
Centre	1,218 33	68 69
Emerald Grove	481 71	45 21
Magnolia	575 00	33 72
Brodhead	100 00	20 00
Monroe	2,638 34	38 52
Albany	950 00	39 46
Geneva	608 35	134 43
Genoa	350 00	73 00
Delavan	400 00	341 18
Allen's Grove	-------	76 00
Elkhorn	1,188 50	35 33
Whitewater	69 00	82 25
Troy	982 25	63 32
East Troy	561 41	103 43
Lafayette	785 84	43 25
Spring Prairie	100 00	3 50
Stoughton	741 50	32 50
Newark, extinct	240 00	7 07
Exeter, extinct	440 00	6 51
Sugar Creek, extinct	175 00	3 17
Clinton	--------	7 07
Beloit, 2d Congregational	--------	8 00

Mineral Point Convention.

CHURCHES.	TOTAL AID.	TOTAL CONTRIB.
Shullsburg	$1,742 50	$59 50
Monticello	742 50	59 50
Darlington	915 71	21 39
Elk Grove	879 16	220 46
Boner Branch	512 50	70 91
Platteville	141 65	270 49
Hazel Green	570 83	98 31
Fairplay	1,733 37	156 69
Lancaster	1,302 09	91 25
Beetown	--------	--------
Patch Grove	1,758 84	83 58
Muscoda	835 00	8 50
Potosi	1,557 00	26 83
Rockville	400 00	5 00
Mineral Point	990 09	79 35
Dodgeville	1,794 95	121 10
Wyoming	1,052 12	72 35
Dover	275 00	29 50
Arena, extinct	175 00	5 00
Pleasant Hill	950 00	12 50
Orion	495 00	6 75
Buena Vista	1,096 67	83 10
Richland City	75 00	3 00
Rugglesville, extinct	100 00	--------
Willow Springs, extinct	280 38	16 50
Yellow Stone, extinct	58 34	--------
Ridgeway P., extinct	433 50	44 00
Dayton	220 00	2 50
Avoca	500 00	6 62
Boscobell	477 50	11 63
Argyle, extinct	94 47	--------
Wyota, extinct	41 68	--------

Madison Convention.

CHURCHES.	TOTAL AID.	TOTAL CONTRIB.
Madison	$118 75	$120 47
Sun Prairie	936 13	60 11
Windsor	525 00	32 54
Black Earth	783 75	17 75
Palmyra	2,079 12	100 86
Fort Atkinson	1,320 47	122 50
Koskonong	433 33	12 00
Lake Mills	....	....
Waterloo	550 00	28 30
Beaver Dam	74 88	213 27
Jefferson, extinct	415 25	6 43
Oak Grove	1,350 00	101 50
Lowell	....	....
Fox Lake	987 67	92 59
Hustisford	....	....
Mazo Manie	200 00	8 50
Wyocena	1,802 87	54 14
Prairie du Sac	1,854 32	71 49
Watertown	1,239 92	189 81
Middleton	457 50	10 75
Spring Green	240 00	34 00
East Ithica	233 37	7 00

La Crosse Convention.

CHURCHES.	TOTAL AID.	TOTAL CONTRIB.
La Crosse	$1,425 00	$243 75
Sparta	1,033 35	31 17
Viroqua	787 50	13 65
Black River Falls	1,650 00	16 30
Prairie du Chien	1,425 00	26 00
De Soto	56 50	....
Trempeleau	1,174 83	37 75
Eau Claire	931 66	26 50
North Pepin	550 00	20 25
River Falls	575 00	78 32

La Crosse Convention.

CHURCHES.	TOTAL AID.	TOTAL CONTRIB.
Prescott	75 00	40 75
North La Crosse	249 99	12 00
Barre	166 66	3 00
Onalaska	249 99	3 00
Hudson	472 02	18 00
Hammond	935 00	22 25
Burns	633 83	7 00
Leon	150 00	3 00
Menomenee	250 00	....
Sterling	137 50	3 50
Malone	50 00	....

Lemonweir Convention.

Saxville	$ 96 33	$5 00
Auroraville	267 17	4 99
New Lisbon	366 67	5 34
Mauston	450 00	2 84
Necedah	450 00	2 84
Westfield	550 00	8 79
Quincy	317 00	....
Roch a Cree	266 63	....
Chester	713 33	5 50
Richford	475 00	2 22
Plover	137 50	....
Tomah	434 55	2 00
Kilbourn City	142 33	....
Lyndon	25 00	....
Merrimac	46 88	3 28
Reedsburg	....	....
Baraboo, C.	....	....
Newport	483 33	13 00
Wautoma	1,466 00	23 07
Grand Rapids	300 00	5 00
Jacksonville	137 50	1 00
Oxford	....	....

Winnebago Convention.

CHURCHES.	TOTAL AID.	TOTAL CONTRIB.
Fond du Lac	$433 37	185 40
Fond du Lac, Plymouth	......	94 50
Ripon	903 49	44 44
Alto	491 61	19 00
Waupun	981 66	146 52
Teycheda, extinct	591 67	13 00
Rosendale	450 00	38 75
Springvale	1,266 67	118 00
Oakfield	1,264 17	55 29
Sheboygan	102 25	133 62
Sheboygan Falls	1,499 75	52 84
Plymouth	902 67	92 45
Oshkosh	891 67	70 52
Waukaw	783 34	24 94
Vinland	325 00	10 00
Neenah	2,082 54	68 31
Pakwaukee, extinct	958 33	6 50
Green Lake	459 50	66 25
Brooklyn	616 08	31 50
Princeton	1,225 00	20 37
Menasha	1,889 96	64 63
Stockbridge Indians, extinct	529 17	14 24
Two Rivers	1,427 90	124 94
Maple Grove	383 33	17 00
Green Bay	......	336 02
Howard	602 08	55 47
Appleton	1,527 08	175 53
New London	905 75	10 50
Hortonville	784 42	38 79
Byron, extinct	250 00	10 55
Empire, extinct	......	......
Metomen	181 92	5 91
Menekaune	475 00	11 00
Oconto	375 00	5 86
Stockbridge C.	250 00	10 58
Waupun Holland	26 25	......

Synod.

CHURCHES.	TOTAL AID.	CONTRIB.
Milwaukee, 1st Presbyterian	$........	$121 17
Barton	1,818 50	89 33
Cottage Grove	1,700 00	169 23
Columbus	1,823 50	90 69
Lodi	1,266 67	33 16
Leeds	747 62	12 50
Lowville	747 63	12 50
Berlin	1,900 00	184 58
Waupaca	2,499 00	9 04
Manitowoc	1,610 66	152 80
Stevens Point	1,592 00	10 00
Baraboo	1,517 19	73 06
Omro	1,655 43	27 00
Markesan	1,104 02	31 16
Poysippi	329 17	26 38
Columbus, German	375 00	8 65
Ashippun	278 83	13 32
Arlington	75 00	35 40
Otsego	250 00	9 25
Pardyville	312 50	11 75
Caledonia	312 50	8 09
Loganville	450 00	3 13
Lawrence	213 33	1 30
Milwaukee, Holland	100 00	....
Rural	1,404 00	29 50
Montello	225 00	8 13
Sun Prairie	50 00	15 00
Jefferson	700 00	10 00
Wausau	766 67	8 00
Portland	158 50	5 87
Scott	120 75	25

Foreigners.

CHURCHES.		TOTAL AID.	TOTAL CONTRIB.
Delafield,	Welch	862 50	70 25
Pike Grove,	"	519 50	31 15
Racine,	"	537 17	55 50
Bark River,	"	360 41	4 66
Mil., Cal. Meth.,	"	858 30	71 27
Emmett,	"	401 16	19 00
Ixonia,	"	605 34	24 50
Spring Green,	"	763 68	19 00
Dodgeville,	"	420 00	26 13
Bethel,	"	420 00	26 12
Welch Prairie,	"	532 35	18 50
Ridgeway,	"	321 33	22 27
Rosendale,	"	150 00	13 60
Oshkosh,	"	424 00	24 10
Milwaukee, C.,	"	528 63	23 50
Blue Mounds,	"	321 34	16 00
Bangor,	"	237 50	9 50
S ring Water,	"	245 00	23 14
Rehoboth,	"	616 25	48 64
Fish Creek,	"	75 00	....
Germans,	total	3,000 32	51 15
Norwegians,	"	875 00	23 00

The whole amount of yearly appropriations and contributions for ten years to the 1st of May, 1861, is as follows:

	APPROPRIATIONS.	CONTRIBUTIONS.
1851..................	11,066 16	789 22
1852..................	13,805 60	667 03
1853..................	13,958 48	898 49
1854..................	14,683 84	1,264 41
1855..................	13,442 25	1,655 62
1856..................	13,600 47	3,057 29
1857..................	16,610 58	2,307 87
1858..................	15,299 07	1,648 86
1859..................	18,846 43	1,695 58
1860..................	15,469 38	2,774 46
	$148,776 26	$16,831 77
German and Norwegian....	3,875 32	74 15
	152,651 58	$16,905 92
Previous to 1851..........	65,000 00	
	$217,651 58	

Many missionaries, especially those who were just entering the ministry and were commissioned to come West with a view of occupying the waste places, were furnished with means to meet the expense of coming; add to this the salaries and expense of Agencies and the whole amount of Home Missionary Appropriations to Wisconsin, from the first, will exceed two hundred and thirty thousand dollars.

FEMALE BENEVOLENCE

Towards Home Missionaries.

The activity of ladies at the East in making up clothing for the families of missionaries, deserves an honorable notice in this connection. They have anticipated and provided for their wants in a manner and measure truly and largely benevolent. The aid thus extended has been timely and most acceptable. The missionaries and their families feel very grateful for it. Many have been relieved of burdens and cares in this way when all other means of relief seemed to be beyond their reach.

In a new country like this where so many duties devolve on missionaries, and where household cares press so heavily on the mother, it is a great relief to receive the yearly box of ready made clothing, prepared, as in many cases they have been, with special reference to them.

By this means, not only are their hearts made glad but their usefulness much increased, and thus Christian females far away are workers together, with those who are here, in the missionary field.

This quiet way of doing good, peculiar to the true woman, is of great value to the cause of Christ, and will in no wise fail of a reward.

CHURCH ERECTION.

The usefulness of missionaries, and the prosperity of the churches, depend so much on their accommodations for holding meetings, that the erection of houses of worship seems to be intimately connected with the history of Home Missions.

Previous to 1857, the number of church edifices erected by the churches embraced in that history, was forty-five, many of them were small and cost but little, being designed for use only a few years, until larger and better ones could be built.

In building those houses but little aid was received from abroad, no arrangements having been made to meet that department of wants.

The origin of the whole church erection movement which has produced large results the past ten years, it is believed, may be found in the liberality of a benevolent gentleman residing in New Haven, Ct. By him the sum of five hundred dollars was placed in the hands of the agent of Home Missions in Wisconsin, to be donated in sums of fifty or one hundred dollars to churches to aid them in building houses of worship.

The results of that investment were so gratifying to the donor, that it was repeated, and a like sum was again donated to be disposed of in the same way. The stimulus thus applied, and the hope thus awakened resulted in the appointment, by the General Convention in 1852, of a Board of Trustees of Church Erection to receive and appropriate Funds. Soon after that the Fifty Thousand Dollars

Fund was raised by Congregationalists at the East, eight thousand dollars of which were given to churches in this State. Since then other sums have been raised at the East and among ourselves.

Presbyterian churches at the East soon engaged in the same benevolent work, and have aided churches in Wisconsin connected with the General Assembly.

The whole number of meeting houses built in the State since 1850, by churches of the denominations that have co-operated in the work of Home Missions here is one hundred and thirty-two. For a more specific statement, see the summary at the close of the following table.

TABLE

Of the houses of worship in 1850, showing when they were built, the material, size, sittings, cost, and aid received.

NAMES.	WHEN BUILT.	MATERIAL.	SIZE.	SITTINGS.	COST.	AID.
Allen's Grove,	'47	w	25x40	250	$800	....
Beaver Dam,	'47	w	26x32	200	800	....
Beloit, 1st C.,	'44	s	38x56	400	4,000	....
Beloit P.,	'50	s	46x70	400	6,000	....
Berlin,	'50	w	24x42	225	350	....
Delavan,	'48	w	32x46	200	1,000	....
Dodgeville,	'48	w	30x40	200	1,000	....
East Troy,	'48	w	25x30	150	....	....
Elk Grove,	'48	w	26x36	200	750	....
Fairplay,	'48	w	26x36	150	800	....
Fond du Lac,	'49	w	30x40	200	900	....
Genesee,	'50	w	37x45	200	1,200	....
Geneva,	'41	w	26x36	150	500	....
Green Bay,	'38	w	40x60	300	3,000	....
Hazel Green,	'48	w	36x46	300	1,600	....
Janesville,	'49	b	50x50	300	3,000	....
Johnstown,	'50	w	32x48	300	1,600	....
Kenosha,	'44	w	40x60	400	4,200	....
Lisbon 1st,	'50	w	30x40	200	700	....
Madison,	'46	w	32x40	250	1,800	....
Milton,	'42	w	20x30	150	500	....
Milwaukee, P.,	'43	w	42x60	400	4,700	....
Milwaukee, Ply.	'50	b	56x100	850	12,500	....
Milwaukee, Free	'48	w	43x60	450	3,000	....
Mineral Point,	'44	w	44x50	350	3,000	....
Mt. Zion,	'44	w	26x36	160	600	....
New Diggings,	'44	w	24x36	150	500	....
N. Rochester,	'49	w	30x43	200	1,000	....
Oshkosh,	'50	w	25x30	150	600	....
Pike Grove,	'46	w	26x36	160	....	....
Platteville,	'46	b	40x60	400	3,000	....
Potosi,	'50	b	25x30	200	1,000	....
Racine, P.,	'42	w	30x60	450	1,000	....
Racine, C.,	'50	w	40x66	600	4,500	....
Raymond,	'48	w	30x38	200	800	....
Ridgeway, P.,	'50	w	20x30	100	400	....

Houses of Worship.

NAMES.	WHEN BUILT.	MATE-RIAL.	SIZE.	SIT-TINGS.	COST.	AID.
Rochester,	'48	w	32x45	300	1,800	....
Salem,	'50	w	16x35	125	500	....
Sheboygan, C..	'47	w	25x32	250	1,200	....
Sheboygan, P.,	'50	w	20x50	200	700	....
Summit,	'44	w	25x40	150	800	....
Troy,	'48	w	38x40	300	1,400	....
Waukesha,	'48	w	26x60	350	2,000	....
Watertown,	'50	w	32x68	200	1,500	....
Whitewater,	'48	b	40x60	450	4,300	....

Houses built since 1850.

NAMES.	WHEN BUILT.	MATE-RIAL.	SIZE.	SIT-TINGS.	COST.	AID.
Allen's Grove,	'54	w	36x55	330	2.000	670
Albany,	'55	w	37x50	250	2,600	200
Appleton,	'53	w	40x84	400	3,500	600
Avoca,	'60	w	24x36	200	700	100
Baraboo, C.,	'52	b	.....	200	1,000	208
Beaver Dam,	'51	w	40x60	350	2,900	...
Beetown,	'51	w	25x35	175	400	...
Beloit, 2d C.,	'59	w	32x50	275	2,800	...
Barre,	'59	w	20x34	100	300	...
Blakes' Prairie,	'55	w	30x42	200	1,400	300
Black Earth,	'61	w	32x50	250	1,300	300
Black R. Falls,	'59	w	21x39	125	800	256
Bristol,	'53	w	32x46	250	1,400	361
Brodhead,	'61	w	36x56	...	2,000	...
Brookfield,	'54	w	34x40	200	1,600	200
Burlington,	'52	w	40x70	300	2,500	200
Caledonia,	'55	w	30x40	200	1,300	200
Centre,	'55	w	25x36	150	865	144
Chester,	'59	w	18x26	100	600	175
Clinton,	'60	w	34x56	280	2,000	...
Delavan,	'55	w	42x70	475	5,050	...
Darlington,	'57	w	.....	250	1,754	125
Dartford,	'58	w	32x42	200	1,200	200
De Soto,	'60	w	24x48	160	1,650	500
East Troy,	'57	w	36x70	400	7,000	600
Elk Grove,	'58	w	32x46	200	1,500	100
Elkhorn,	'58	w	30x48	250	1,400	...

Houses of Worship built since 1850.

NAMES.	WHEN BUILT.	MATERIAL.	SIZE.	SITTINGS.	COST.	AID.
Emerald Grove,	'54	w	26x45	200	2,000	500
Evansville,	'57	b	.....	225	2,500	...
Eau Claire,	'59	w	41x64	300	3,500	250
Fort Atkinson,	'52	w	36x47	400	3,000	...
Fulton,	'58	b	36x55	300	2,800	...
Fox Lake,	'55	w	28x38	150	1,500	200
Fond du Lac, Pl.	'57	w	35x60	300	2,000	...
Geneva,	'51	w	40x60	400	2,500	...
Green Lake,	'55	w	34x40	150	1,200	175
Hartford,	'54	w	32x50	250	1,700	225
Hartland,	'57	b	28x42	200	1,900	200
Hortonville,	'59	w	24x44	160	1,600	...
Howard,	'55	w	26x45	150	1,000	...
Hudson,	'59	w	35x55	300	2,000	250
Jamestown,	'60	w	32x40	200	1,100	...
Jenkinsville,	'61	s	36x40	200	1,300	...
Koskonong,	'61	w	28x44	200	1,000	...
Lake Mills,	'52	b	32x40	200	1,300	130
Lancaster,	'51	w	30x40	175	1,000	125
Lafayètte,	'60	w	28x42	225	1,400	257
La Crosse,	'55	w	28x75	300	2,060	...
Madison,	'58	b	42x74	500	4,400	...
Mazo Manie,	'58	w	.....	125	1,150	175
Menasha,	'58	w	36x56	275	3,000	300
Milton,	'57	b	34x50	200	1,500	200
Mil., Hano. st.,	'59	w	48x80	600	7,360	5455
Mil.. Spring st.,	'57	b	64x96	1100	30,000	...
Magnolia,	'54	w	34x52	300	1,065	200
Monroe,	'60	w	35x45	200	1,400	200
Neenah,	'59	b	38x50	150	2,000	208
New London,	'60	w	36x56	280	2,000	500
Oak Creek,	'55	w	31x52	225	1,650	225
Oak Grove,	'54	b	32x44	200	3,000	200
Oakfield,	'53	w	24x36	100	650	275
Oconomowoc,	'54	w	32x50	300	2,500	225
Oshkosh,	'57	w	60x95	700	10,000	...
Palmyra,	'55	w	30x50	250	2,300	200
Union Grove,	'51	w	30x40	160	600	...

Houses of Worship built since 1850.

NAMES.	WHEN BUILT.	MATERIAL.	SIZE.	SITTINGS.	COST.	AID.
Pewaukee,	'55	w	30x50	240	$700	150
Pleasant Pra.,	'58	w	31x48	200	2,000	...
Pleasant Hill,	'56	w	32x40	160	800	125
Plover,	'54	w	28x36	200	400	...
Plymouth,	'59	w	32x47	225	1,400	250
Pra. du Chien,	'58	b	36x50	250	2,800	1,039
Pra. du Sac,	'51	w	28x52	200	1,000	...
Prescott,	'56	b	36x50	300	4,000	200
Princeton,	'54	w	26x36	250	600	250
Racine, P.,	'52	b	59x90	800	12,000	...
Racine, C.,	'52	b	-----	500	7,350	300
Ripon,	'53	w	30x46	300	800	50
River Falls,	'55	w	30x50	150	1,600	300
Rockville,	'53	w	18x36	125	300	95
Rosendale,	'55	w	34x48	250	1,600	150
Reedsburg, C.,	'55	w	32x50	250	1,500	200
Salem,	'51	w	26x35	125	500	150
Sheb. Falls,	'55	w	40x60	300	3,000	225
Shopiere,	'52	s	40x56	300	3,000	175
Shulsburg,	'52	s	35x45	300	2,000	150
Sparta.	'57	w	36x55	250	3,100	1,000
Spring Prairie,	'60	w	32x50	200	1,800	...
Springvale,	'55	w	32x44	175	1,200	200
Sun Prairie,	'60	w	24x44	150	1,200	100
Two Rivers,	'58	w	36x50	150	1,000	200
Stone Bank,	'58	w	26x32	125	600	...
Trempeleau,	'57	w	28x36	150	1,350	200
Waupun,	'52	w	32x44	400	1,000	350
Wautoma,	'56	w	30x40	150	1,100	194
Waterford,	'58	w	36x56	350	3,800	100
Westfield,	'61	w	28x48	300	1,000	200
Wauwatosa,	'53	w	41x64	450	3,347	225
West Salem,	'60	w	26x48	300	1,000	150
Wilmot,	'54	w	32x40	200	1,200	300
Williams,	'58	w	32x48	180	3,000	150
Wyocena,	'55	w	36x45	260	2,000	200
Windsor,	'60	w	30x40	200	1,500	...

Welch Houses of Worship.

NAMES.	WHEN BUILT.	MATERIAL.	SIZE.	SITTINGS.	COST.	AID.
Milwaukee,	'58	w	26x40	180	1,375	100
Oshkosh,	'56	b	.....	200	1,500	300
Spring Green,	'55	w	22x26	130	620	...
Spring Water,	'56	l	18x24	60	80	...
Bangor,	'59	w	28x36	160	800	150
Blue Mounds,	..	w	20x28	150	475	100
Racine,	'56	b	.....	150	700	100
Welch Prairie,	'50	w	22x25	100	450	...
Cambria,	'60	w	34x45	200	1,100	...
Ridgeway,	..	w	21x18	100	175	...
Delafield,	..	w	18x28	130	.....	...
Bethel,	..	w	.....	...	300	...
Dodgeville,	..	w	.....	...	500	...
Pike Grove,	'53	w	.....	...	400	...
Bark River,	'59	w	.....	...	400	75
Ixonia,	'56	w	.....	...	300	...
Rosendale,	..	l	.....	...	.....	...
Rehoboth,	..	l	.....	...	.....	...
Fish Creek,	..	..	None	...	.....	...
Emmet,	..	..	None	...	.....	...

Summary of Church Erection.

Whole number of houses of worship in 1850........	45
Whole number of houses of worship built since 1850..	120
Total..................................	165
Whole cost of the 45............................	$85,800
Whole cost of the 120...........................	$249,076
Total..................................	$334,876
Aid in building the 45..........................	$1,325
Aid in building the 120.........................	$22,991
Total aid..............................	$24,316
Received from the Congregational Building Fund...	$12,442
Received from churches and individuals East and West, and from the Board of Church Erection of the Convention.........................	$13,220
Whole number of church bells....................	34
Total weight....................................	27,763lb
Total cost......................................	$10,532
Whole number of sittings........................	40,600
Houses built of wood............................	139
Houses built of brick...........................	21
Houses built of stone...........................	5
Houses enlarged.................................	12
Houses being built..............................	6
Houses built by churches that had small ones before..	10
Churches that have none.........................	44

APPENDIX.

New School Presbyterian Synod of Wisconsin.

The following statements and statistics relative to this Synod are given mainly because of their relation to the work of Home Missions the past ten years in the State.

They are placed in an appendix for reasons assigned in the preface.

They are given chiefly on the authority of brethren, who have kindly responded to circulars that were sent to them; some were taken from the minutes of the General Assembly, and some from documents of the Home Missionary Society.

They do not include churches or ministers located in the region of Lake Superior, but some other churches are included, though not connected with this Synod, and for the same reasons that some churches are included in the statistics of the Convention, though not in fact connected with it.

The entire history of this Synod, and of the Presbyteries of which it is constituted, is included in the ten years over which this work extends.

When the former history of churches in Wisconsin was published, there was no other organization than the Presbyterian and Congregational Convention, which sustained a relation to the A. H. M. Society.

Early in 1851, the question of a separate organization was agitated, chiefly by brethren who had but recently come to the State. Some who were connected with the Convention, and some who were already here but had formed no connection, united with them. Some of the churches belonging to the Convention went with their ministers; other churches have since been organized, and other ministers have come in and united.

Organization of Presbyteries.

The Presbytery of Milwaukee was organized early in 1851, and composed of Rev. Wm. H. Spencer, Rev. Eli S. Hunter, D. D., and Rev. Mr. Steele, ministers; and the First Presbyterian Church in Milwaukee, and a newly organized church at Walker's Point in Milwaukee.

The Fox River Presbytery was organized in the Autumn of 1851, and was composed of Rev. C. E. Rosenkrans, Rev. J. B. Preston, and Rev. Cutting Marsh, ministers, and the churches of Columbus and Berlin.

In 1856, the Presbytery of Columbus was organized. The number of ministers and churches in Fox River Presbytery had increased, and the bounds were so wide that a division took place, and one portion took the above name.

The Synod was organized in 1857, and was composed of all the ministers and churches connected with these three Presbyteries.

In 1856, an Agent of Home Missions was appointed by the Church Extension Committee of the General Assembly, whose labors were chiefly those of exploring the field, and organizing or securing the organization of churches in that connection. His services were continued a year or more, and resulted in the addition of a considerable number of churches to the Synod. Since then there has been no agent of that Committee in the field.

The churches thus organized were most of them small and feeble. They have been aided, with few exceptions, in the support of ministers by the American Home Missionary Society.

For the most part the churches and ministers of the Synod have co-operated with the Society, in good faith, as it is believed, to the present time, and a disposition has been evinced on the part of the Society to aid and foster them, the same as those of the Convention.

The following tables contain the principal statistics of ministers and churches in that connection, and their houses of worship.

Ministers.

In collecting materials for this work, circulars were sent to ministers of Synod the same as to those of the Convention; but on making out the tables of statistics it was found impracticable to include all the particulars. Those contained in the following tables are supposed to answer the main design as it relates to Home Missions, and as the returns in some cases were not full, and the tables would necessarily be imperfect, only a part of the statistics are given.

The following table contains first, the names of ministers of this connection now in Wisconsin, their native State, when they came, and their present fields of labor; and next, the names of those who have been in the State some portion of the past ten years, when they came, where they labored, when they went away, and also those who have died. Both these last named will be found also in tables with others on pages 77 to 80.

Ministers.

TABLE:

Containing the names of ministers now in Wisconsin, their native State, when they came, and their fields of labor.

NAMES.	NATIVE STATE.	CAME TO WIS.	FIELDS OF LABOR.
W. M. Adams,	Ohio,	1861	Beloit,
S. H. Ashmun,	N. Y.,	1851	Rural and vicinity,
S. H. Barteau,	N. Y.,	1852	Pardyville and Wyocena,
J. Conly,	Ireland,	1855	Ashippun & Stone Bank,
J. H. Dillingham,	N. Y.,	1860	Manitowoc,
W. Drummond,	Scotland	1846	Portland and Waterloo,
A. G. Dunning,	N. Y.,	1855	Arlington,
G. W. Elliott,	....	1853	Milwaukee, City Miss.
C. Hall,	....	1857	Colporteur,
C. F. Halsey,	N. Y.,	1858	Wausau and vicinity,
J. C. Holmes,	N. J.,	1852	Maple Grove,
M. Holmes,	N. J.,	1854	Sabbath School Miss.
J. G. Kanouse,	N. J.,	1846	Cottage Gro. & Sun Pra.
J. N. Lewis,	N. Y.,	1851	Without charge,
J. S. Lord,	Conn.,	1857	Barton & Scott,
H. T. Lothrop,	Mass.,	1850	Palmyra,
C. Marsh,	....	1836	Without charge,
J. B. Preston,	....	1850	Omro,
F. B. Reed,	....	....	Without charge,
B. G. Riley,	N. Y.,	1858	Lodi and vicinity,
E. F. Waldo,	N. Y.,	1857	Jefferson,
T. Williston,	N. Y.,	1858	Reedsburg & Loganville,
C. Ven de Ven,	Holland,	....	Milwaukee, Holland ch.,
P. Zonne,	Holland,	....	Holland, Sheboygan Co.

Ministers.

Ministers who have been in Wisconsin and have left,—when they came, where they labored, and when they went away; also those who have died.

MINISTERS.	CAME.	WHERE LABORED.	WENT AWAY.	
A. Eddy,	1849	Beloit,	1856	Ill.,
W. Bridgeman,	1859	Waupaca & Plover,	1860	......
C. R. French,	1852	Barton & vicinity,	1857	Iowa,
H. Gregg,	1857	Baraboo,	1859	Ohio,
W. Herritt,	1849	Manitowoc Co.,	1853	Ill.,
M. Kidd,	1855	Walker's Point,	1856	Ill.,
P. Kanouse,	1854	Cottage Grove,	1856	N. J.,
W. Lusk,	1857	Reedsburg,	1859	Ohio,
W. A. Niles,	1850	Beaver D. & Watert'n,	1859	N. Y.,
L. Rood,	1856	Omro,	1859	N. Y.,
S. G. Spees,	1856	Milwaukee,	1859	Ohio,
W. H. Spencer,	1850	Milwaukee,	1856	Phil'd.
Mr. Steele,	1851	Walker's Point,	1852	N. Y.,
J. Willson,	1853	Milwaukee,	1855	Ind.,
Ch. Wiley,	1856	Milwaukee,	1857	......
S. Uhlfelder,	1857	Loganville,	1859	Iowa,
Oswald,	1856	Columbus, Ger.,	1857	Iowa,
E. S. Hunter,	1851	W. C., Died in	1858	......
J. D. Strong,	1856	Lowville, Died in	1859	......
C.E.Rosenkrans	1842	Columbus, Died in	1861	.. ...

Of these forty-four ministers, thirty-one have labored under commissions from the American Home Missionary Society.

Of the twenty-four now in the State, seventeen are supplying twenty-five churches, several of which are in connection with the Convention, and ministers belonging to the Convention are supplying several of the churches connected with Synod.

TABLE :

Containing a list of churches,—when organized, members then, members now, houses of worship, when built, and their cost.

CHURCHES.	WHEN ORG.	MEMBERS THEN.	MEMBERS NOW.	HOUSES OF WORSHIP.	
				WHEN BUILT.	COST.
Ashippun,	1857	8	18	building	....
Arlington,	1855	10	19	none,	....
Baraboo,	1851	14	67	1852	unknown
Barton,	1852	12	30	1853	1,100
Berlin,	1850	23	78	1856	4,500
Caledonia,	1857	10	22	none,	....
Columbus,	1850	17	57	1854	1,400
Columbus, Ger.,	1856	..	..	....	....
Cottage Grove,	1846	23	40	1860	1,200
Eaton,	1858	..	..	....	....
Hampdon,	1851	..	..	....	....
Holland,	....	..	40	....	....
Jefferson.	1858	11	29	building	....
Lawrence,	1856	5	12	none,	....
Leeds,	1858	14	15	none,	....
Lodi,	1852	10	80	1859	2,500
Milwaukee, Hol.	....	..	150	....	....
Loganville,	1857	7	8	none,	....
Lowville,	1851	9	20	none,	....
Markesan,	1847	7	20	1857	2,650
Manitowoc,	1851	15	30	1855	800
Maple Grove,	1852	14	43	1858	800
Milwaukee,	1837	in 1850 175	306	1843	6,000
Montello,	1858	12	26	none,	....
New Lisbon,	1858	..	..	....	....
Omro,	1852	..	80	none,	....
Otsego,	1856	..	..	....	....
Pardeeville,	1857	7	36	none,	....
Poisippi,	1853	8	30	none,	....
Portland,	1858	11	26	none,	....
Reedsburg 1st,	1857	7	24	1858	1,800
Reedsburg 2d,	1858	6	3	none,	....

CHURCHES.	WHEN ORG.	MEM-BERS THEN.	MEM-BERS NOW.	HOUSES OF WORSHIP.	
				WHEN BUILT.	COST.
Royalton,	1860	..	..	none,	....
Rural,	1858	9	24	1860	1,400
Scott,	1858	10	12	none,	....
Stevens Point,	1852	5	..	1855	1,600
Sun Prairie,	1858	32	31	1859	600
Waupaca,	1851	..	20	none,	....
Wausau,	1858	5	8	none,	....
Beloit,	1849	in 1850 100	150	1850	6,000

Of these forty churches, six were organized previous to 1851, four of them belonged to the Convention, and two of them, when organized, were Congregational. Three others, organized since, were Congregational.

Three of the forty support their ministers without aid, viz:—Milwaukee, Beloit and Berlin. Thirty-one are, or have been aided by the A. H. M. Society. Six are believed to be extinct. A few are supposed to be aided now by the Church Extension Committee, and all are supplied, at least a portion of the time.

By the table on page 109, it will be seen that the amount of aid granted by the A. H. M. Society to churches of this connection, in the support of their ministers, is $26,113,47, and the amount contributed to the Society by all the churches of Synod, for the same time, is $1,212,24.

Fifteen of these churches have houses of worship, and besides these, the two Holland churches are supposed to have houses. Some of these houses are yet unfinished, though occupied. Two or three others are being built.

The aggregate membership of the churches, so far as known, is about fifteen hundred.

Other Denominations.

Efforts made to obtain information relative to the full evangelical religious strength in Wisconsin have not been successful. The last reports published, so far as can be ascertained, give statistics as follows :

OLD SCHOOL PRESBYTERIANS.

One Synod and three Presbyteries—39 ministers, including absentees ; churches, 49 ; members........... 2,000

EPISCOPALIANS.

Parishes, 44 ; rectors or ministers, 46 ; members...... 1,800

REGULAR BAPTISTS.

Churches, 199 ; ministers, 130 ; members.............. 9,026

EPISCOPAL METHODISTS.

Circuit preachers, 201 ; local preachers, 300 ; members, 17,000

DUTCH REFORMED.

Churches, 7 ; ministers, 5 ; members................. 1,000

WESLEYAN AND PROTESTANT METHODISTS.

Circuits, 20 ; ministers, 41 ; members................ 1,200

SEVENTH DAY BAPTISTS.

Churches, 10 ; ministers, 17 ; members............... 1,100

There are many other smaller denominations among Americans. Among the Welch there are three or four ; among the Danes as many, and among the Germans many ; some of which appear to be evangelical; very many do not.

Adding to the above the members connected with the Convention and the N. S. Presbyterians, and the whole number of members will be, nearly, 50,000

www.ingramcontent.com/pod-product-compliance
Lightning Source LLC
LaVergne TN
LVHW021419110826
845150LV00007B/1993
* 9 7 8 1 4 2 5 5 0 8 8 7 6 *